PH2T3R

THE JOURNAL OF SOLAR CULTURE

VOLUME 1

WRITTEN BY
THE FIRST MEN

THE ORDER OF FIRE

ARIZONA 2024

PH2T3R: The Journal of Solar Culture
Volume 1, 2024

Edited Jack Donovan.
Typesetting and Cover Design by Jack Donovan.

Contributing authors: Jack Donovan, C.B. Robertson, Ed Hamann, Dustin Lindsey, Taylor Martin, Paul Bicknell, Paul Begadon, Madison Rubin, Juan Pablo Midence, Vic Verdier, Mark Kelley, Christopher Healey.

Published by The Order of Fire LLC. Gilbert, Arizona.

Order of Fire LLC
Mailing address:
18521 E Queen Creek Rd STE 105-133
Queen Creek, AZ 85142

Orderoffire.com
theorderoffire@gmail.com

ISBN: 979-8-218-36475-5

TABLE OF CONTENTS

DESCENDING ODIN'S THRONE

LYRICS + POETRY

TABLE OF CONTENTS

ABOUT THIS JOURNAL
JACK DONOVAN

First, the name...

I heard that if you spell a word funny, the kids will think it's cool.

Proto-Indo-European is the theoretical root language of all Indo-European languages, living and dead. In Proto-Indo-European (PIE), the reconstructed root that means "father" is *ph₂tḗr*. The "*h₂*" indicates a sound that is uncertain and disputed among linguists. The most reasonable, accessible, and up-to-date guess I found in my research for writing this explanation is that *h₂* sounds something like the "h" in the Arabic pronunciation of the word "Muhammad."

I was brainstorming a name for a cultural project to bring the ideas in Fire in the Dark to life.

Since there was already a number in the word *ph₂tḗr*, I decided to point toward the future and spell "father" in "code."

Like a password. PH2T3R.

When I commissioned the logo for PH2T3R, I told the graphic designer that I saw PH2T3R as a "cultural engine of creation." He brilliantly managed to come up with something retro-futuristic that looks like both the sun and a gear.

I created the PH2T3R website shortly after *Fire in the Dark* was published and started by writing articles for that site, some of which are included here in the first printed volume of this journal. The PH2T3R project commissioned a sculptural solar mandala and several musical projects and maintained an Instagram page, which began to feature AI artwork inspired by solar themes. I somehow became an early adopter of AI art technologies, starting with some programs built on Google and moving immediately to MidJourney when it first launched.

I founded The Order of Fire in response to a reactionary wave of Christian conversions in the men's space in 2021 and 2022. I reached out to friends and associates – guys who were on the same page as I was regarding what I have called the "Hliðskjálf dilemma." Men interested in myth and religion but too self-aware and realistic to convince themselves the one god or pantheon of gods represented the absolute truth.

The Order of Fire opened to the public through an application process around October of 2022, and we welcomed several of our first members, many of whom are still with us today and some who have work included in this book.

The Order of Fire has two primary missions.

1. To encourage excellence in men and help its members become the best versions of themselves.
2. To create and promote a new Solar Culture, as described in "The Manifesto of Solar Culture" (which follows the Introduction).

Under the name PH2T3R, I released three collaborative musical compositions, with more to follow. The first was "Crossing the Night Sea," commissioned through PH2T3R as a soundtrack for Solar

Meditation. Original Order member Fredrik Hejdenberg composed a second meditation track titled "Solar Wind." Fredrik and I later collaborated on an orchestrated mythic speech titled "Invocation of the Storm."

Fredrik also collaborated with original Order member Paul Begadon to produce "Into the Light," a musical argument for studying the heroic stories of the past. The lyrics are included in this volume, followed by lyrics that Paul wrote for original Order member Kyle Brickell's musical project, Sol Anahata.

As the organization evolved, we started producing collaborative podcasts and videos for YouTube discussing philosophical and historical subjects using the name PH2T3R: THE JOURNAL OF SOLAR CULTURE.

This journal is a physical record of the same process of thought and creation.

It begins with some foundational texts that can also be found online – "The Manifesto of Solar Culture" and "The Name of the Dragon is Negation."

This Journal puts into print several expositions by our resident blue-collar philosopher, C.B. Robertson, including his opus, "Descending Odin's Throne," composed specifically for this volume. I also wrote a couple of new essays for the book.

The remaining meat of this Journal of Solar Culture is a record of essays, research, and creative writing projects produced by members of the Order during its first twelve months of existence. You'll find everything from the poetry of Madison Rubin and Juan Pablo Midence – both farmers, incidentally – to our Vedic guru Ed Hamann's treatise on ghee. I've also included essays by members Vic Verdier, Dustin Lindsey, Paul Bicknell, and Taylor Martin.

They say that everything on the Internet lives forever. And perhaps it does – somewhere. But you have to know it exists and where to look for it. I have been writing online long enough to see essays, articles, posts, and pictures become nearly impossible to find. People close accounts, stop paying for hosting or intentionally delete websites. A physical publication is still a more reliable record. Part of this publication's purpose is to document our movement's history.

So, for the record, this has been a movement of both words and actions.

Members of the Order gathered officially for the first time in December 2022 in Boise, Idaho, where we practiced jiu-jitsu together with the help of black belt Paul Sharp and finished a dinner with our first Holy Round.

In March 2023, I led a group of men out into the Arizona desert to perform the first Fire Ritual, modeled after the myth of the First Men from *Fire in the Dark*. We camped overnight and kept watch over the fire until the sun rose the following day. Our Northeastern group performed a ritual over the same weekend.

In April 2023, European members of The Order of Fire met in London to visit the Mithras Temple and the British Museum's Mesopotamian and Sutton Hoo exhibits.

In June 2023, similar Fire Rituals were performed in British Columbia and Australia with members of the Order.

In September 2023, our members traveled to Las Vegas and performed a Fire Ritual in the Nevada desert.

In October 2023, I traveled to Ireland, where I visited the ancient sites of Newgrange and Knowth with European members of the Order of Fire, and we performed a Fire Ritual in the rainy Irish countryside.

In December 2023, I traveled to Georgia to perform the first Fire

Ritual involving firearms and a salute to the sun for the winter solstice.

Shortly after this journal is published, our members will meet again in Arizona to perform our second Fire Ritual there.

Various groups of our members have gathered and visited historic places and hiked and trained together all over the world during that time. Men are physical beings, and it is action in the physical world that separates history from fantasy.

While I am proud of this journal and the many discussions and expressions of solar creativity that the Order has facilitated and inspired over the past year or so, we are still deep in our blue hour.

This Journal of Solar Culture will ignite curiosity and creativity, and there will be more thinking, writing, and doing. There will be more solar music, poetry, and art.

The culture of The First Men will grow and reproduce itself and expand its influence. And, in some unknowable elaborated future form, the light of our fire will break past the hazy purple horizon of what we are able to dream in the present and reveal a way forward for countless men yet unborn.

I'll see you there, Bvlls.

Stay Solar –

Jack Donovan, Editor
February 2024, Arizona

PH2T3R

THE JOURNAL OF SOLAR CULTURE

THE MANIFESTO OF SOLAR CULTURE
JACK DONOVAN

Definition brings things into being — gives them shape and form and separates them from the raw chaos of the undifferentiated and undefined.

Fire in the Dark gestured at a new, syncretic culture of manly idealism assembled from our Hliðskjálfum — our high seats — from which we can look out upon all of known human history and assess it and recognize patterns and synthesize it into a forward-facing culture for men of the future.

But that was only a gesture, a quick scribble to describe motion, mood, position, and form. More work must be done to transform the gesture into a sketch, the sketch into a drawing, the drawing into a painting, and the painting into a masterpiece.

The answer to Nietzsche's question, "What festivals, what sacred games shall we have to devise?" has just been asked and has yet to be answered. There is much to do!

So, for several months now, I have been speaking amongst friends — my Bulls! — about solar idealism and the solar culture it demands. It has become clear that to bring solar culture into being, we must better describe what it is. And when we have said what solar culture is, then we shall also know what it is not.

SOLAR CULTURE

Solar Culture looks first to the sun and the sun's dynamic, controlled fire for its inspiration.

Solar Culture idealizes the sun as a source of light that makes knowledge and reason possible, that makes distinction and differentiation and order possible.

Solar Culture idealizes the sun as a source of gravity that pulls things into His orbit, and as a source of warmth and nourishing light that cause all within His circle to flourish. The Sun is leadership, and the symbol of fathers and kings beyond fathers and kings.

Solar Culture acknowledges man as an animal of flesh and bone, the most conscious of many creatures under the Sun who benefit from His light.

Solar Culture is inspired by the primal, archetypal past and the myths and aesthetic elements from historical cultures. The challenge of Solar culture is to remix the primal, mythic past and synthesize it into a vision of the future. Solar culture is forward-thinking and future-primitive.

Solar Culture aims to synthesize the myriad manifestations of the masculine archetypes identified as The Father, The Striker, and the Lord of the Earth, elucidate their aspects, natures, and domains, and invoke them via every available media.

Solar Culture recognizes the power of individual and group rituals for the human animal and intends to articulate new ritual architectures that direct the emotions and unconscious realities of man toward his highest potential.

Solar Culture aims to breathe new life into old myths and archetypes by recreating them with living hands and eyes and making them relevant again to new and future generations.

Solar Culture explores themes of light over darkness, order over chaos, truth over falsehood, health and vitality over sickness, beauty over ugliness, strength over weakness, courage over fear, competence over incompetence, fortitude over fragility, emotional control over hysteria, and self-determination over servility.

Solar Culture reveres and cherishes the feminine insofar as it is faithful to, aligned with, and supportive of Solar Order.

Young men are lured to cultures and aesthetics of darkness because they know instinctively that it is part of their role as men to encounter darkness, and it is their encounter with darkness that will define them — as we know all heroes in relationship to the names of the dragons they have slain. But, in seeking the darkness that defines the light, men must be reminded that their role is to overcome darkness and not allow it to overcome them.

Aesthetically, Solar Culture aims to uplift. Solar Culture is characterized by a dynamic gravitas, by brightness and action, by nobility and virility.

When Solar Culture explores darkness, chaos, and anti-virtue, it does so in the context of identifying its opposite. Render the dragon of negation as a formidable opponent, but a dragon to be controlled and battled against — never worshipped or glorified. Solar Culture does not luxuriate in the abyss.

Solar Culture is not meant to criticize — it is not an argument. Solar culture is the positive act of creation that follows a constellation of conclusions.

In the unfinished and abstract, Solar Culture aims to communicate action, integration, and coming into being rather than disintegration, collapse, disease, and decay.

All desolation is a stage for becoming.

As we encounter new and unforeseen aspects of darkness, new dimensions and boundaries of Solar Culture will be revealed.

This manifesto is meant only to begin the conflagration of creativity, to ignite a movement — as an Order of Fire emerges from the darkness.

For men of the future...

PH2T3R

THE JOURNAL OF SOLAR CULTURE

THE NAME OF THE DRAGON IS NEGATION
JACK DONOVAN

Most creation stories begin in a realm of perfect equality — in a formless, non-differentiated void in which everything has the same value.

Enuma Elish — Mesopotamian Creation Myth

When the heavens above did not exist,
And earth beneath had not come into being —
There was Apsû, the first in order, their begetter,
And demiurge Tia-mat, who gave birth to them all;
They had mingled their waters together
Before meadow-land had coalesced and reed-bed was to he found —
When not one of the gods had been formed
Or had come into being, when no destinies had been decreed,
The gods were created within them

Book of Genesis — King James Bible

In the beginning God created the heaven and the earth.

And the earth was without form, and void; and darkness was upon the face of the deep. And the Spirit of God moved upon the face of the waters.

And God said, Let there be light: and there was light.

And God saw the light, that it was good: and God divided the light from the darkness.

And God called the light Day, and the darkness he called Night. And the evening and the morning were the first day.

From the Rig Veda

There was neither non-existence nor existence then; there was neither the realm of space nor the sky which is beyond. What stirred? Where? In whose protection? Was there water, bottomlessly deep?

There was neither death nor immortality then. There was no distinguishing sign of night nor of day. That one breathed, windless, by its own impulse. Other than that there was nothing beyond.

Darkness was hidden by darkness in the beginning; with no distinguishing sign, all this was water. The life force that was covered with emptiness, that one arose through the power of heat.

In the Germanic literature there was *Ginnungagap*, and the first being was the possibly "non-binary" Ymir. In the Mesopotamian version, Tiamat was a chaotic mother-monster who, like Ymir, must be destroyed by the first Striker, in this case Marduk, who then ascends to become the Father/King who creates the known cosmos from the corpse of the chaotic beast.

Creation begins when the first Striker slays the first Chaos dragon.

"(h_1e) *gwént $h_1$ógwim*." (He killed the serpent)

In the biblical sense — though that is not my specialty — I suppose that one could say that God "killed" chaos, or the void, by breaking it with light and causing differentiation, and by introducing reason or *logos* via the Word.

There are so many frames and ideologies and of course the details of things always involve paradoxes and complications. But if one were to condense all of these teachings and find the similarities and overlapping truths, one could say that most of our ancestors associated goodness and creation with differentiation, and evil and death with non-differentiation.

There are a some other stories that seem to contradict this, but for the most part, the pattern of differentiation vs. non-differentiation is relatively consistent.

Consider the symbol of the dragon or the serpent — or the devouring monster or *Jotun* — and what it does or threatens.

It comes from the darkness of the earth and threatens death by poison or consumption or (in later stories and our modern tales) a reduction to ash by fire. Death is a return to dirt, a return of the differentiated, conscious being to undifferentiated matter.

Ashes to ashes and dust to dust.

Our story — all of our romance and art and poetry — requires the dragon and is fundamentally *about* our relationship with the dragon.

The dragon and the chaotic void beyond its gnarled and gaping maw represent the negative polarity that requires a positive response. Light is meaningless without darkness and it is the absence of order which stimulates order.

It is through interacting with chaos and contending with it conceptually or physically that we grow.

Chaos contains all of the raw materials for creation. We reach into it like a sculptor scooping clay from the earth and we shape it according to our will.

As creatures of the earth, we can reconnect with the void and flirt with it and experience "oneness" through various ecstatic, Dionysian practices involving drugs or dance or sex, or even through mob movements in which we disappear into the "all that is one."

To remain solar champions of light and life and order, the festival must end, and we must return from the void to the ordered world and resume our fated struggle to differentiate and maintain the differentiation that makes all meaning and valuation and narrative possible. We can access and experience the void, but if we refuse to beat it back and allow it to overcome us like an opiate — if we allow ourselves to disappear into it, in a sense, we are "already dead."

However, one must admit that the Dragon does have a certain charm.

Sometimes a man who goes out to hunt the Dragon ends up having a conversation with him, and the Dragon attempts to convince him that the struggle of men has always been absurd.

The Dragon, chewing playfully on his own tail, tells the man that the all is truly one, and that Enlightenment is the realization that nothing matters, because everything is fundamentally the same. All names are changeable and all boundaries are tenuous and fragile. All life will end. Every law will eventually be broken and every reputation will eventually be forgotten. The Dragon explains that the most eternal truth is negation — which also happens to be the Dragon's name — and when he says this, the man knows that he is not telling a lie.

The man slumps down and holds his head with his hands and he despairs.

The Dragon comforts the man by reminding him that, so long as he is alive, he can experience pleasure and sensation. He tells him that the gift of life is experience, and that experience and sensation are all that matter.

This uplifts the man's spirit, and he leaves the Dragon, whose name is Negation, and he abandons all attachment to meaning and returns to the world of light and differentiation as a servant of the void.

The man spends the rest of his life seeking sensation above all else, and says whatever he needs to say to continue having pleasing experiences, because he now believes that all things are the same and all boundaries between right and wrong and good and evil are illusory and temporary.

The servant of the Dragon may seek sensation and experience through deception and violence or he may seek it peacefully, depending on his nature.

The message of Negation can be as comforting as the womb and the embrace of death.

Often, when a man has not sought out the Dragon, the message of the Dragon is first whispered to a man by a woman.

Imagine there is nothing to protect, nothing to fight for, and that nothing is sacred. Just relax.

"Why not eat the apple... or open the box..."

The idea that nothing matters is the most freeing, most feel-good sentiment in the world — because it absolves men of all duty and responsibility.

"And the world can live as one..."

Perfect "oneness" is death — the loss of all distinct identity and differentiation.

The "ego" and the "I" disappears into the "we" or the "it," and finally, the "nothing" that is "everything" all at once.

All ashes and dust...

If the servant of the Dragon wishes to be seen as wise, he repeats the message of the Dragon.

Many believe the servant of the Dragon, and together they all laugh at the men who work so hard to separate the sacred from the profane and maintain the boundaries that make all meaning and valuation and narrative possible.

The Dragon's truth is not a lie — though it is far easier to call the Dragon a liar.

And perhaps it is wiser to do so...to tell a noble lie by calling the Dragon a liar.

Bright men tend to project their interest in and aptitude for investigating truth outward universally onto those who demonstrate far less aptitude and little or no such interest.

The differences between the truth of Negation and the truths of men are differences of scale and of time.

What matters, and when does it matter?

Does what you create matter, even though one day it will certainly be destroyed?

Does beauty matter, even though it will one day become ugly or be erased?

Does value matter, even though all things come from and will return to the void — eventually rendering them all equal in value?

Does the way in which you conduct yourself matter — even though within in a few generations (or sooner), it is likely that no one will remember your name?

When you fight Negation, you fight it for the moment or the decade or the century, but when driven backward, he retreats to the vault of his black casino and sleeps on his mountain of gold peacefully, knowing that the house always wins.

Perhaps this is the true meaning of the serpent that coils around the sun disk on the crown of Ra. Light and life and solar order are contained and surrounded by the serpent and the void, in the way that a midnight fire is contained by a darkness that patiently waits for it to burn out.

When the Dragon or one of his servants speaks to us and tells us the truth of Negation, we can choose to follow them into the darkness and chaos where all meaning and differentiation disappear.

We can become psychopaths or slippery nihilists who speak prayers laced with the language of love as they worship nothing.

The alternative is to commit to the present and the immediate future at human scale — to commit to this living, breathing manifestation of the eternal.

To recognize that nothing will ever be more real to us than our lives and nothing can ever mean more to us than the things to which we assign the highest value.

To insist on meaning and differentiation because it matters to us and to the people we care about and because we revere the perilous beauty of it.

To continue to create that which will ultimately be destroyed and order that which will at some point again become disordered.

Because we are finite beings who inhabit the present and are gifted with consciousness and the ability to perceive and create like mortal gods.

The void is indifferent. Nature is indifferent.

We can choose to be indifferent and follow the dragon into the abyss, or we can choose to determine for ourselves...

"what matters — and when?"

THE WORLD NEEDS A HERO
AND IT MUST BE YOU
DUSTIN LINDSEY

Part of the beauty of the four-week challenge[1] we all undergo is how each facet synergistically contributes to the others. By cutting out political and current events media streams, I've needed something to fill that void; in the mornings, during my workouts, this is either music or the Aeneid, both of which I've committed to for my challenge. During the evenings, this is reading fiction to help calm myself down as part of my evening routine – namely, a compilation of all the stories of Robert E. Howard's Conan the Cimmerian.

The parallels between ancient and modern myths are well-documented. Authors and academics such as Joseph Campbell have written ad nauseam about the connections in the human psyche which we all share, from which these myths spring. This led Campbell in particular to formulate a quantified Hero's Journey which (almost) all myths share. However, I believe Campbell, though arguably brilliant, was missing the point. He was too swept up in the cultural tides of his day. The sexual revolution was in its infancy when he wrote the Hero With a Thousand Faces, and it shows; his apparent obsession with the psychosexual detracts significantly from the bigger picture which he tries to paint. And this bigger picture also misses the forest for the trees: rather than attempting to find the deeper meaning from which these myths spring, he tries to declare that the fact that we share mythological roots in our psyches can only mean that we are all "one" as a human race. This sort of silly universalism was, again, a product of the era of hippies, free love, and John Lennon proselytizing about abolishing violence and borders while simultaneously beating his wife.

Despite all this, there is value in the concepts which Campbell established. Heroes play an extremely important role for us as men. Whether this hero is Gilgamesh, Siegfried, or Indra is dependent on the region and the culture from which these myths arose, but their purpose is clear: it gives us an example to live up to. Many heroes, such as Achilles, are inherently flawed, but the flaws are not what we attempt to emulate; rather, they establish a heroic ideal, something which cannot be reached, but to which we aspire regardless of our limitations in order to make our lives worth living. Alexander the Great famously (allegedly) slept with a copy of the Iliad beneath his pillow, and his campaigns were, according to many historians, his attempt to live up to the legend of Achilles. By looking to heroes as an example, as our journeys take us through our own archetypal heroic cycles, we have a roadmap we can use to accomplish great things.

There is an issue, however, with classical canon. While the ideals remain timeless, and many in the Order of Fire can speak to these ideals in much greater depth than I can, the characters themselves exist in a world which differs greatly from our own. The way in which their cycles take shape were informed by the culture in which those who told the stories existed. For example, the Iliad was sung in a time when Greek city-states regularly went to war with one another, and most young men participated in battle at some point in their lives. These battles weren't quite as lethal as we know them now, but the risk of death was certainly there, and looking to Diomedes for inspiration certainly had its place. The Odyssey is slightly more applicable, in that young men can certainly spend time adventuring, as I do and fully intend to continue doing; but while much of the world is unknown to us, it is certainly not unexplored, and none of us can expect to find cyclopes lurking in caves (although some of the people I've met in bars on the road might meet that description).

This is not to say that these stories are not invaluable. They are and should remain an essential part of any curriculum, particularly that of what we are trying to build here. However, we are not ancient Greeks. We must bring the past forward.

Robert E. Howard is one of the greatest examples of this. Modern myth (by which I mean contemporary, not the ideology of modernism), while lost in today's Imperial propaganda arm known as Hollywood, still has a valuable place in forming our aspirational goals outside plastic popular culture. Conan the Cimmerian gives us, in the form of stories which are relatively young, a heroic journey which we can emulate. His world is semi-fictitious, but having been written by a modern man, is informed by a world which we know and understand. His character traits, though flawed, give us an example to which we can aspire. There are no demons to slay with phoenix-hilted swords, but there are certainly demons within each of us which we must conquer in order to prosper. Training seriously with battle axes would be silly in today's world, but we can and should train to achieve as close to physical perfection as we can. There are no wizards to battle, but we can and should battle the "magics" and manipulations of the Empire in our own lives, so that we may spread the Light and Order of the Sun in order to improve the lives of our loved ones and positively contribute to the world around us.

This is where there is a void which the Order of Fire can and should fill. Whether it is in music or writing, many of us have talents with which we can contribute to the artistic world. We are already making great strides in this direction, and I am extremely proud to be witness and party to it. But we must remember that what we are writing are the myths which will be passed down to future generations. We are creating what men in years and decades to come will aspire to become. By living our lives according to Solar Idealism and creating our myths in accordance with this ancient Tradition, we can and will bring the past forward, and slowly but surely, we will create a world in which our progeny will prosper. We will plant the seeds of trees beneath whose shade we know we will never sit, because we can, and we must.

And if in the process I end up looking like a Frazetta painting, you certainly won't find me complaining.

Editor's Note

1   Dustin was one of the first members of the Order of Fire, and in the early
months, we had a 4-week challenge instead of a 3-month challenge.

HANDSHAKE WITH DAVID
TAYLOR MARTIN

The biblical account of David defeating Goliath in the Old Testament is one that remains very popular and well-known today, even outside of Christianity. The young shepherd boy with his simple sling faces off against the mighty Phillistine giant who wields a javelin twice the size of his opponent. With divine intervention at his side, David hurls a stone, striking Goliath in the head, knocking him to the ground. The head of the beast is severed, hoisted in the air to the cheers of the onlooking Israelites. It's the original underdog tale. It is a lesson of courage that says through faith, one can overcome what seems impossible.

The West today is seemingly full of young men who, to me, seem like Davids. Frail, slaves to trends, and with penchants for hubris. I see a lot of them out and about where I live. I like to think that the absurdity of the socio-political world the last few years has made many of them wake up, to steal the popular phrase, from this evolutionary retrograde the world seems to be stuck in. Hopefully, I'm right. But in any case, they aren't ripping the heads off of giants.

There's some Goliath's out there too, though few and far between compared to the Davids...and they definitely aren't losing to a young punk with a slingshot.

Jack Donovan's 2012 hit *The Way of Men* was a wake-up call for many men around the world. It was an acknowledgement that the problems they could sense with the modern world, and men's place in that world, were not misplaced. One of its key themes was that men from all cultures, races, and creeds look for the same qualities in other men because at our most basic, primal level, we needed those qualities in other men in order for the tribe to survive in our pre-modern times. Those qualities are pure and universal.

I read Jack's book when I was 17 and I definitely had some "David" qualities about myself at that time. However, I understood innately what it attempted to communicate. It wasn't saying anything you or I didn't already know, it affirmed feelings we'd had for a long time.

I've had the great opportunity to talk with Jack personally and when recounting my introduction to his work, he replied, "It's hard to connect to the young guys." That has stuck with me. I'm at the very tail-end of the Millennials. The Zoomers of Gen-Z probably consider me an old man, yet the vast majority of the population would consider me young at 28. I've made it a point to try and strike up conversations with younger guys at the gym, at work, at social gatherings, etc. It is extremely strange to be just old enough to have watched social media and technology destroy the average person's social skills. It's detrimental to our civilization. Forming new, real, physical and social bonds in this technological age is not easy, yet you have to try.

But it's also very clear to anyone paying attention that Gen-Z, who have grown up with cell phones and social media being a part of their everyday lives, communicate and socialize very differently than generations before them. They are a completely different people... and their children will be even further removed. I can't recall the number of times I've reached out my hand for a shake when introducing myself to a Zoomer and they react like I just offered them meth. If I have trouble connecting to guys barely 10 years younger than myself, well...no wonder Jack said that.

The Order of Fire aims to produce new and meaningful culture that emphasizes "...the masculine archetypes identified as The Father, The Striker, and the Lord of the Earth, elucidate their aspects, natures, and domains, and invoke them via every available media." So, what do we, the men who have chosen to illuminate the darkness of this world, do about this connection problem with the young men who have not yet found the higher path? Do we give up and isolate ourselves so that the fire dies with us when we pass on? Do we just hope that another man comes along in 200 years and re-rewrites *The Way of Men* all over again? Of course not, that wouldn't be very solar.

Let's keep it real; the journey in addressing this issue starts with those around your campfire, kith and kin. To steal the famous Jordan Peterson quote, "Before trying to save the world, try cleaning your room first." Make sure you and your spouse/partner are on the same life mission. Raise strong and competent children. Keep your friends honest and accountable, and be loyal to all of them. Organize those things first and you're bound to have good results. That's where most of us should probably be spending the majority of our time. As for the rest of the lot...

It's very easy for people of my cohort and especially those of older ones to discount the current population, aged 20 and below, as completely lost causes. They have no communication skills, their obsessed with social issues, they're not interested in traditionally masculine activities, they're all gay or trans, and on and on. And most of that is probably true to some degree for a lot of them. But there's also a good chance there are a few out there who see through all the deceit, the shamelessness, the degeneracy. They are aching for someone to tell them there is a better way to be, a way that always was and always is. 1 in 4 Gen-Z adults have said that they spent some part of their teen years talking to a therapist (Cox, et al., 2023). What if they just had someone take them camping in the forest?

I'm not going to tell you to just start tossing out copies of Gary Paulsen or Jack London novels (or even *The Way of Men*) and tell them to figure it out. Like anything else that the Order of Fire creates in alignment with Solar idealism, this endeavor requires physical intent and action, like stoking the flames of a fire. I won't prescribe an exhaustive list of to-do's and certainly each person is going to have different needs but you don't have to think very hard about this stuff either. Humans are innately observational creatures; we learn by watching and imitating what others do and say.

Be a role model for the young men around you. In your family, friend group, your colleagues and acquaintances, even for the strangers observing from the sidelines. Show them the benefits and importance of being strong, both physically and mentally. Offer to take them hunting or fishing and teach them how to harvest game. Give them books that aren't preachy but full of ancient life lessons and wisdom – men need stories of overcoming and conquering challenges. Show them how to properly dress themselves. Encourage them to never stop their education. Introduce them to beautiful and transformative art. Show them what it means to be loyal to your friends. Show them what honor looks like. Show them what living SOLAR looks like.

Let them know that you also don't have all the answers, but that you are always trying to learn from better men around you.

David defeating Goliath is a feel-good underdog story, but it isn't the way the world works. Imagine an alternate scenario. Goliath acknowledges the guts it took for the little pipsqueak to stand up to him in the first place. He lays down his spear and extends a hand of camaraderie instead. David reciprocates the gesture and two go off to get jacked and tan and conquer the next city over. Why be the lone wolf when you could have a gang of barbarians? Sounds like a more interesting tale to me. In fact, I think I just described The Epic of Gilgamesh to some degree. There are probably many things the Goliaths of the world could teach to the young men around them, and they need to.

Don't get me wrong, this isn't going to work on everyone. There are a lot of guys out there that just won't get it or refuse to do so because of some misinterpreted, self-righteous feeling they have about why masculinity and living strong for life is bad. That's fine. Not everyone gets to ride this party bus. They can fit in or fuck off. But there are a lot of David's out there who would make great allies, better yet, friends.

We were lucky to have the inspirations in each of our lives that drove us to become better versions of ourselves. Whether it was a personal father figure, a sports coach, or a really good book, it doesn't matter. We should not assume the next generation will have such luck. Don't toss the young men of the world today away. Many of them are Goliaths inside and they are the next caretakers of the campfire.

STAY SOLAR

SOLAR IDEALISM; A SOLUTION TO SOCIAL DECLINE
PAUL BICKNELL

Introduction

A recent poll by Gallup[1] found that 54% of Americans believe that the state of moral values in the U.S. are poor, and 83% consider those values to be in decline. Another series of studies[2] appear to show that individuals in around 60 nations harbor a general belief that moral values are in decline.

Whether or not these individuals' beliefs are in fact illusory is difficult to definitively say. However, if true, they indicate a majority perception of a society in moral decay. Whilst it may be difficult to measure a decline in moral values, it is difficult to disagree with the surveys' findings - given the emerging seemingly disorientated culture of "trending" crowd and media driven hysteria, hollow virtue signaling and participation trophies, to name but a few. The above indicates a direction of travel toward a society devoid of something worthy, noble, excellent; something ideal – a society lacking meaning or purpose; a state of moral and even existential nihilism, alienation or disillusionment.

This social decline is not new, for example, Nisbet (1962)[3] observed:

> "[...]it has become steadily clearer to me that alienation is one of the determining realities of the contemporary age: not merely a key concept in philosophy, literature, and the social sciences (making obsolete or irrelevant many of the rationalistic premises descended from the Enlightenment) but a cultural and psychological condition implicating ever larger sections of the population. By alienation I mean the state of mind that can find a social order remote, incomprehensible, or fraudulent; beyond real hope or desire, inviting apathy, boredom, or even hostility. The individual not only does not feel a part of the social order; he has lost interest in being a part of it. For a constantly enlarging number of persons, including, significantly, young persons of high school and college age (consider the impressive popularity among them of JD Salinger's Catcher in the Rye), this state of alienation has become profoundly influential in both behavior and thought. Not all the manufactured symbols of togetherness, the ever-ready programs of human relations, patio festivals in suburbia, and our quadrennial crusades for presidential candidates hide the fact that for millions of persons such institutions as state, political party, business, church, labor union, and even family have become remote and increasingly difficult to give any part of one's self to."

Solar Idealism and Solar Culture[4]

The conflict between societal decline and advancement outlined above represents a conflict between meaning and meaninglessness. Perhaps you, the reader, have observed this conflict as Nisbet did, and countless others, both on a social and individual level.

The Solar Idealist views this state of nihilism as an opportunity; a liberative platform from which to create and advance a new system of strong values; values that have stood the test of time. Friedrich Nietzsche articulated this opportunity in the context of a breakdown in collective religious social values of relevance here:

> "In fact, we philosophers and "free spirits" feel ourselves irradi-
> ated as by a new dawn by the report that the "old God is dead";
> our hearts overflow with gratitude, astonishment, presenti-
> ment and expectation. At last the horizon seems open once
> more, granting even that it is not bright; our ships can at last put
> out to sea in face of every danger; every hazard is again permit-
> ted to the discerner; the sea, our sea, again lies open before us;
> perhaps never before did such an "open sea" exist."[5]

Solar Culture continuously synthesis mythological, philosophical,
scientific and other teachings into a vision for the future. A vision of
meaning and purpose that acknowledges but defies nihilism.

A vision that explores themes of: *"light over darkness, health and vi-
tality over sickness, beauty over ugliness, strength over weakness, courage
over fear, competence over incompetence, fortitude over fragility, emo-
tional control over hysteria and self-determination over servility"*,[6] iden-
tifying and bringing together what is best.

Examples of this confrontation between meaning and meaning-
less can be seen in the form of the human struggle against per-
sonal and societal challenges illustrating to us that individuals can
find purpose and meaning by confronting and overcoming those
challenges:

Beowulf

An epic poem set in world of monsters in which the hero Beowulf
demonstrates a defiance to nihilism. His battles against Grendel
and Grendel's mother appear to symbolise the struggle between
order and chaos, meaning and meaninglessness. By facing these ex-
istential threats, the hero asserts his agency bringing with it order,
purpose and meaning to his life and those of others.

Theseus and the Minotaur

Theseus, the hero, enters the Labyrinth to face the Minotaur. Similar to Beowulf, his determination to confront a terrifying adversary exemplifies the capacity for individuals to find purpose by conquering their fears and challenges, over acceptance, passivity and meaninglessness.

The Epic of Gilgamesh

The hero, Gilgamesh goes on a quest for immortality, reflecting a desire to overcome the apparent meaninglessness of human existence – what's the point if we are going to die. This quest illustrates man's longing for meaning and significance. Gilgamesh does not achieve physical immortality and this forces him to grapple with the realities of his existence, teaching him to confront it and as a consequence, lead him to a finite life of purpose and meaning.

The Odyssey

This features the hero, Odysseus, who is presented with the option of immortality by Calypso, but rejects it in favour of returning to his family. This suggests to us that there is greater value in connection and richness in the human experience over a seemingly endless existence lacking depth or significance.

Conclusion

It is through the teaching of these old stories, and philosophies that we can learn to understand and confront the problems prevalent in today's world – through Solar Culture, these problems can be overcome. Solar Culture continues to reveal itself as a golden thread of morality in the fabric of society, ascribing, meaning, purpose and definition to life; and with it an antidote to nihilism.

Notes

1   Brenan, M. (2003) "Views of State of Moral Values in U.S. at New Low", Gallup.com. However, it is not clear on the exact number of individuals surveyed. Of course, these beliefs are opinions, which themselves could be misguided, and there does not seem to be a consensus as to how this decline can be objectively measured.

2   Mastroianni, A.M., Gilbert, D.T. (2003) "The illusion of moral decline." Nature 618, 782–789, which reviewed a number of surveys administered to people around the world between 1949 and 2021.

3   Nisbet, R. (1962) "Community and Power" (formerly the Quest for Community). Oxford University Press, at viii.

4   See Donavan, J. (2022) "The Manifesto of Solar Culture", The Journal of Solar Culture, for an explanation of Solar Idealism and Solar Culture.

5   Nietzsche, F. (1882) "The Gay Science". Random House.

6   Donavan, J. (2022) "The Manifesto of Solar Culture", The Journal of Solar Culture, for an explanation of Solar Idealism and Solar Culture.

THE CATTLE OF THE SUN
SOLAR SPIRITUALITY AS "DUE RESPECT" IN HOMER'S ODYSSEY
C.B. ROBERTSON

The Sun is owed respect — that is my essay.

For thousands of years, the image of the sun has inspired men to emulate it, to shine forth like an undeniable force of power and beauty in the eyes of other men. For many young men seeking to establish themselves, this solar imperative appears as a desire to oppose the powers that be, like a young wolf challenging an old alpha. This adversarial approach is ancient, as is the mythical image of an antagonist seeking to "devour the sun."

But there is an equally ancient view that approaches solar spirituality in a different manner. We see this approach depicted in Homer's *Odyssey*, one where solarity is not achieved by adversarial conflict, but rather through deference and respect.

Homeric epic followed (or rather set) the rules we see in modern copywriting, where a summarizing headline precedes a somewhat more expressive subheading, an explanatory summary of an opening paragraph, and only then a chronological account of the actual story. According to Dr. Gregory Nagy, it was proper form for the epic poet to summarize the thematic content of the entire poem in the opening lines:

The singer was following the rules of his craft in summing up the whole song, all 100,000 or so words, in one single word, the first word of the song [...] We see from the beginnings of both the Iliad and the Odyssey that the rules of the singer's craft extend beyond the naming of the main subject with the first word. In the original Greek of both the Iliad and the Odyssey, the first word announcing the subject–Anger, Man–is followed by a specially chosen adjective setting the mood: disastrous anger, versatile man. This, in turn, is followed by a relative clause that frames the story by outlining the plot–the disastrous anger that caused countless pains, the versatile man who wandered countless ways.

Though Odysseus "suffered many pains, heartsick on the open sea" – from Polyphemus the cyclops to the sorceress Circe; from the tantalizing sirens to the deadly gap between Charybdis and Scylla; from the narcotic trap of the Lotus Eaters to the cannibal Laestrygonians – only one challenge is mentioned in the opening lines of the epic: the Cattle of the Sun.

> Sing to me of the man, Muse, the man of twists and turns
> driven time and again off course, once he had plundered the hallowed heights of Troy.
> Many cities of men he saw and learned their minds,
> many pains he suffered, heartsick on the open sea,
> fighting to save his life and bring his comrades home.
> But he could not save them from disaster, hard as he strove—
> the recklessness of their own ways destroyed them all,
> the blind fools, they devoured the cattle of the Sun
> and the Sungod wiped from sight the day of their return.
> Launch out on his story, Muse, daughter of Zeus,
> start from where you will—sing for our time too.
> (Odyssey 1)

In the Greek, the Odyssey opens with "ἄνδρα" (andra, "man") and establishes the primary theme of the story. Of the challenges faced by this man, the summarizing opening lines speak only of the devouring of the cattle of the Sun. This suggests that this episode is either the most significant challenge, or else symbolically summarizes all of the other challenges faced by "the man."

From this, what comes into focus is a story of the relationship between man, the sun, and cattle, one which illustrates both what is meant by the "cattle of the sun" and what Homer believed to be the proper relationship between Man and the Sun. The *Odyssey* offers a path of spiritual guidance, a starting place for "solar spirituality" as understood by the priests and artists of the bronze age, but which can only be understood by connecting with these opening passages.

Only by learning the language — and therefore the minds — of the ancients will they be able to sing for our time too.

CATTLE

Cattle have long been associated with various "sky-father" deities. From as early as the reconstructed Indo-European cosmogenesis story featuring the sacrifice of a cosmic cow, cattle have been identified not merely as sacrificial animals, but as animals associated with and set aside for the Gods.

As introduced by the opening lines of the Odyssey, the cattle referenced in "the cattle of the sun" represented a much broader symbol to the Greeks, a stand-in for the belongings of the gods or of the respect owed to the gods.

We see reinforcements of this understanding in two examples: first, in the Promethean origin of Greek sacrificial practice, and second, in the story of the Minotaur of Crete.

From Hesiod's *Theogony*, we hear the story of how Prometheus tricked Zeus in the sacrifice of an ox:

> For when the gods and mortal men had a dispute at Mecone, even then Prometheus was forward to cut up a great ox and set portions before them, trying to befool the mind of Zeus. Before

the rest he set flesh and inner parts thick with fat upon the hide, covering them with an ox paunch; but for Zeus he put the white bones dressed up with cunning art and covered with shining fat. Then the father of men and of gods said to him: "Son of Iapetus, most glorious of all lords, good sir, how unfairly you have divided the portions!"

So said Zeus whose wisdom is everlasting, rebuking him. But wily Prometheus answered him, smiling softly and not forgetting his cunning trick: "Zeus, most glorious and greatest of the eternal gods, take which ever of these portions your heart within you bids." So he said, thinking trickery. But Zeus, whose wisdom is everlasting, saw and failed not to perceive the trick, and in his heart he thought mischief against mortal men which also was to be fulfilled. With both hands he took up the white fat and was angry at heart, and wrath came to his spirit when he saw the white ox-bones craftily tricked out: and because of this the tribes of men upon earth burn white bones to the deathless gods upon fragrant altars.

This trick subsequently became a precedent for sacrifice, preserving the meat for humans, but still respecting–at least in spirit–a known and established debt to the Gods in cattle.

And indeed, we see a description of this sacrificial method of wrapping bones in fat in the *Iliad*, not as some attempt to trick the Gods, but as custom:

His prayer went up and Phoebus Apollo heard him.
And soon as the men had prayed and flung the barley,
first they lifted back the heads of the victims,
Slit their throats, skinned them and carved away
the meat from the thighbones and wrapped them in fat,
a double fold sliced clean and topped with strips of flesh.
And the old man burned these over dried split wood
and over the quarters poured out glistening wine
while young men at his side held five-pronged forks.
(Iliad 1)

Cattle are not the only animals sacrificed to the gods, but they are the primary and ideal sacrificial animal, and are the sacrificial animals of choice in texts like the *Theogony* and the *Iliad*.

We see this association reinforced in the breach in the story of the Minotaur, as described by Pseudo-Apollodorus, where an attempt to exchange the bull of a God for a man's bull results in disastrous consequences:

Asterius dying childless, Minos wished to reign over Crete, but his claim was opposed. So he alleged that he had received the kingdom from the gods, and in proof of it he said that whatever he prayed for would be done. And in sacrificing to Poseidon he prayed that a bull might appear from the depths, promising to sacrifice it when it appeared. Poseidon did send him up a fine bull, and Minos obtained the kingdom, but he sent the bull to the herds and sacrificed another.

But angry at him for not sacrificing the bull, Poseidon made the animal savage, and contrived that Pasiphae should conceive a passion for it. In her love for the bull she found an accomplice in Daedalus, an architect, who had been banished from Athens for murder. He constructed a wooden cow on wheels, took it, hollowed it out in the inside, sewed it up in the hide of a cow which he had skinned, and set it in the meadow in which the bull used to graze. Then he introduced Pasiphae into it; and the bull came

and coupled with it, as if it were a real cow. And she gave birth to
Asterius, who was called the Minotaur.

(Pseudo-Apollodorus, *Bibliotheca*)

Here the association between the gods and cattle doubles back on
itself; the bull-man that Pasiphaë gives birth to becomes a reminder
of the refusal to sacrifice correctly. The corrupted image of the bull
is associated with a failure of due respect, just as the beautiful and
pure image of the bull is associated with the proper sacrifice, with
favor from the gods, and even with the gods themselves.

As the story of the Minotaur makes clear, the cattle are not fungible.
One cannot swap a beautiful white bull – a bull sent by and reserved
for Poseidon – with an ordinary bull without consequence.

Both the Prometheus and the Minotaur stories illustrate the im-
portance of cattle as a symbol of sacrifice to the gods, rightfully
belonging to them. But they also demarcate the line of distinction
between the cattle of men and the cattle belonging to the Gods. The
Odyssey does not assert this understanding on its own authority, but
rather summarizes a deeper cultural understanding of these beliefs,
depicting them visually as the challenge of the Cattle of the Sun.

THE SUN

Let us turn to the sun.

In the *Odyssey*, the "cattle of the sun" belong to Hyperion/Helios.

The Greeks have at least seven "Solar" deities. Helios is arguably
the most well-known, driving his chariot across the sky every day.
Helios is the son of the Titan Hyperion, who also personifies the Sun
(this distinction is made in later works, but in the *Odyssey*, Hyperion
and Helios are used interchangeably). The Greeks had goddesses as-
sociated with the dawn, with sunrise, and the day – Eos, Elektryone,
and Hemera, respectively. One of the most repeated and famous

epithets in the *Odyssey* – "*Eos rhododactylos*" ("rosy-fingered dawn") – explicitly refers to this Dawn in its personified and divine form. Although primarily a God of thunder, Zeus also has solar associations — the sun is sometimes referred to as the "eye of Zeus." Finally, Apollo is a god of light and vision and is associated with the Sun, and is particularly important as a solar god in the story of the Iliad.

The character of this sun — and thus, of Hyperion — can be seen in aggregate across these solar deities. They are not all alike, but are owed respect in a similar fashion, and one can see the consequences of failure to give this respect in each.

We see, for instance, the the entire conflict of the Iliad instigated by Apollo, after Agamemnon insults one of his priests:

> What god drove them to fight with such a fury?
> Apollo the son of Zeus and Leto. Incensed at the king
> he swept a fatal plague through the army–men were dying
> And all because Agamemnon spurned Apollo's priest.

The primary epithet of Apollo is phoibos, which means "radiant." Apollo is a god of light, as well as poetry, archery, prophecy, and healing. But the earliest depictions associate him specifically with plague and illness, and his role in the spread of illness was the reason Bronze Age Dorians (like the Trojans) appealed to him to rid them of disease. When the priest Chryses prays for redress against the Greeks, Apollo is addressed as "Smintheus, god of the plague."

The solar associations of Apollo appear almost as an addition, like an appellation given to a god who was not solar by birth, but who became solar by virtue of his powers. His skills are wide-ranging and his character complex, reflecting a complex origin and place within the Greek pantheon. Apollo, in other words, was "solar," but not "the sun". His power and beauty made him like the sun in the mind of the Greeks. These qualities render him "radiant."

Beyond the gods, we see this kind of appellation applied to certain mortals, most notably to the most famous warrior in the Iliad:

> Begin, Muse, when the two first broke and clashed,
> Agamemnon lord of men and brilliant Achilles.

The word for "brilliant" in this opening is δῖος (dios), which is variously translated as "brilliant," "shining," "noble," "heavenly," even "god-like." Achilles is not a god, but he has qualities that earn him a "solar" epithet in his poetic depiction.

The solar qualities of Apollo and Achilles are not qualities of being the sun, but are qualities of being like the sun. The primary quality of being like the sun is visible in the epithets ascribed to solar beings: "shining," "radiant," "brilliant." These epithets connote power and beauty that is undeniable, and which is most visible in absentia, as in when Achilles withdraws from the battle, or when Hyperion threatens to withdraw from the sky.

But this distinction between being the sun and being like the sun must not stop us from remembering that nothing is more like the sun than the sun itself. The sun may serve as a metaphorical depiction of greatness, but as a baseline, nothing "solar" supersedes the sun. The sun is both a source of this "brilliant" quality in the beautiful and powerful among gods and men, but is also a stand-in for this very concept of greatness.

THE CATTLE OF THE SUN AS "DUE RESPECT"

With these interpretations in mind — derived both from the structure of the poem and from the broader context of the Greek mythic imagination — a more direct understanding of "the cattle of the sun" comes into view. The "cattle of the sun" can be seen as "respect owed to those like the sun."

We see this theme reinforced throughout the Odyssey.

When Odysseus departs from king Aeolus' kingdom, he is given a bag that contains the winds so that he can sail home smoothly. However, just as he is nearly home and Ithaca's shores are in sight, his companions become suspicious and jealous. They open the bag — believing it to contain treasure — and release the unfavorable winds, blowing them all the way back from to Aeolus again, whereupon the king declares:

> Away from my island–fast–most cursed man alive!
> It's a crime to host a man or speed him on his way
> when the blessed deathless gods despise him so.
> Crawling back like this–
> It proves the immortals hate you! Out–get out!

This reaction illustrates both a violation and an observation of the principle. Odysseus' compatriots fail to trust their captain and disrespect him in the process. They disrespected their superiors who are the relative solar beings and brought misfortune upon themselves. But Aeoleus, sensing the dysfunction, respects the gods and sends them away so their trouble does not spread by association to him.

The most explicit example of this theme of due respect is that of the episode with Polyphemus, the cyclops. After telling the cyclops his name was "Otis" ("no man"), Odysseus and his crew manage to blind Polyphemus and escape his cave. They make it out to the shore, and Odysseus' willingness to shun glory– which is associated with one's name–appears to have paid off, since when the other cyclops ask Polyphemus who has blinded him, all he can say is "no man has done this!"

But when their boat was leaving the shore, Odysseus lost his sense of propriety and respect and began to taunt the blinded cyclops. Even the crew began to check Odysseus:

> They threw themselves in the labor, rowed on fast
> but once we'd plowed the breakers twice as far,
> again I began to taunt the Cyclops–men around me
> trying to check me, calm me, left and right:
> 'So headstrong–why? Why rile the beast again?'

In his hubris, Odysseus revealed his true name. Armed with this name, the cyclops prayed to his father Poseidon.

And so Poseidon delayed Odysseus' homecoming by another decade.

The anger of Poseidon is, in a sense, the reason for the story of the *Odyssey*. It is the reason Odysseus' journey home is an epic story, and not just a few weeks' journey. The *Odyssey* is — distilled — the story of a man who, in his pride, failed to show due respect and was punished for it.

This theme is reiterated ceaselessly across the whole *Odyssey*. We see "due respect" paid to foes by properly anticipating their power and not underestimating them. In anticipation of the Sirens, Odysseus does not trust in his willpower to resist their song, but instead does as he has been instructed by Circe and has his crew tie him to the mast. This is a form of respect; the proper demonstration of respect in this case involves sacrificing personal freedom and autonomy for a brief moment out of an appreciation for the danger he is about to encounter.

By following the formal ritual and showing the proper respect, Odysseus gains insight and wisdom from the seer Tiresias in the underworld. It is notable that in Book 11, the dead seer Tiresias says nothing of the sirens, Charybdis, or Scylla, but warns Odysseus not to harm the "herds and fat flocks, the cattle of Helios, god of the sun who sees all, hears all things."

Despite initial inclinations to fight the monster Scylla, Odysseus obeys Circe's instructions to pass by the cliffs as fast as possible:

'So stubborn!' the lovely goddess countered.
'Hell-bent yet again on battle and feats of arms?
Can't you bow to the deathless gods themselves?
Scylla's no mortal, she's an immortal devastation,
terrible, savage, wild, no fighting her, no defense–
just flee the creature, that's the only way.'

Odysseus wins favor and life itself by his deferential and respectful approach of Nausicaa among the Phaeacians. But the Phaecians paid a price for assisting him; angry Poseidon wrecked the assisting ship and enclosed their port with a mountain, perhaps justifying king Aeolus' refusal to associate with those hated by the gods.

There are also examples of this theme emerging in characters besides Odysseus. Notable examples include the loyalty of the swineherd Eumaeus, and the good manners of Telemachus in Pylos and Sparta. And of course, the nearly superhuman patience and devotion of Penelope. Each of these is rewarded for preserving what belongs to someone else — in this case, not the Sun or another god, but Odysseus.

On the other hand, the *Odyssey* shows two key examples of this principle in violation. The suitors in Ithaca abuse the hospitality of Penelope, wife of Odysseus. Odysseus is not a god, but is loved by Athena, and has solar attributes of his own. For their disrespect, the suitors are eventually butchered in the palace by Odysseus and Telemachus.

But the most critical and first-named example takes place in Book 12 (the significant middle-point in a 24-book poem). Odysseus and his crew, having narrowly survived Charybdis and lost six men to Scylla, come to the island of Thrinacia. Circe had just warned the men to steer clear of there, for the island belongs to the Sun God Hyperion. But if they had to land, they must not touch the God's cattle. Odysseus is outvoted by his men, who insist on landing for a while as a reprieve from the toils of sea. After making his men swear an oath not to touch the cattle, they land. The winds promptly stop,

and after a month trapped on the island, the ship runs out of food
and the men begin to starve. While Odysseus was asleep, the men
decided they'd rather drown then starve to death:

> Listen to me, my comrades, brothers in hardship.
> All ways of dying are hateful to us poor mortals,
> true, but to die of hunger, starve to death–
> that's the worst of all. So up with you now,
> let's drive off the pick of Helios' sleek herds,
> slaughter them to the gods who rule the skies up there.
> If we ever make it home to Ithaca, native ground,
> erect at once a glorious temple to the Sungod,
> line the walls with hoards of dazzling gifts!
> But if the Sun, inflamed for his longhorn cattle,
> means to wreck our ship and the other gods pitch in–
> I'd rather die at sea, with one deep gulp of death,
> Than die by inches on this desolate island here!"

The men captured some of the cattle, killed and ate them, in a sacri-
ficial manner. But as with the Poseidon's bull for king Minos, a sac-
rifice does not serve as atonement and does not justify taking what
belonged to the Sun. When Odysseus awoke, he upbraided his men
for breaking their oath, but there was no way to un-kill the animals.
After a week of eating the god's cattle, the winds returned and the
men set out. But Hyperion threatened to withdraw his sunlight
from the sky if Zeus did not repay the blood with blood. As the men
set out, Zeus darkened the sea and the sky, and struck the craft with
his thunderbolt:

...Helios burst out in rage to all immortals:
'Father Zeus! the rest of you blissful gods who never die–
punish them all, that crew of Laertes' son Odysseus–
what an outrage! They, they killed my cattle,
The great joy of my heart... day in, day out,
when I climbed the starry skies and when I wheeled
back down from the heights to touch the earth once more.
Unless they pay me back in blood for the butchery of my herds,
down I go to the House of Death and blaze among the dead!'
But Zeus who marshals the thunderheads insisted,
'Sun, you keep on shining among the deathless gods
and mortal men across the good green earth.
And as for the guilty ones, why, soon enough
on the wine-dark sea I'll hit their racing ship
with a white-hot bolt, I'll tear it to splinters.'

All aboard died except Odysseus.

HEROIC IDEALISM AND SOLAR IDEALISM

The "due respect" we see throughout the *Odyssey* can be seen as the initial phase of a process by which one achieves a kind of theosis — the transformative union with God or godliness. A similar aspiration is seen in the Iliad, but the approach in the *Odyssey* is very different from that taken by the Iliadic warriors at Troy.

In the Iliad, aspiring warriors pursued immortality by means of what can be called "heroic idealism." To the thumotic young warrior, the stories and songs of great men are, in a sense, more real than the mundane physical reality of life — not merely because real life is mundane, but because it is also transient, whereas great stories offer kleos aphthiton, "unwilting glory," which is never forgotten. The Homeric hero of the Iliad aspires to live in this linguistic domain of glorious song, the price of which is his life... but life is not enough. He must take arms against a sea of troubles, against a force far greater than himself.

The *Iliad* contains numerous passages in which a character becomes daimoni isos, "equal to a god," but this moment of glory is usually achieved by challenging a god, and almost always immediately anticipates death:

> Three times Patroclus charged the jut of the high wall,
> three times Apollo battered the man and hurled him back,
> the god's immortal hands beating down on the gleaming shield.
> Then at Patroclus' fourth assault like something superhuman
> [īsos daimōn],
> The god shrieked down his winging words of terror: "Back–
> Patroclus, Prince, go back! It is not the will of fate
> that the proud Trojans' citadel fall before your spear,
> not even before Achilles–far greater man than you!"

Patroclus is pursuing the heroic glory of the Iliadic hero by antagonizing a God, who — upon the fourth charge — kills Patroclus. In this way, Patroclus achieves heroic immortality, alongside Achilles, in the greatest epic poem in the Western tradition.

But in the *Odyssey*, we see signs of uncertainty over the desirability of this aim, or at least of this method. When Odysseus meets Achilles in the underworld, the greatest of the Iliadic heroes expresses deep regret over this path:

> I reassured the ghost, but he broke out, protesting,
> 'No winning words about death to me, shining [*phaidim*] Odysseus!
> By god, I'd rather slave on earth for another man–
> some dirt-poor tenant farmer who scrapes to keep alive–
> than rule down here over all the breathless dead.'

Perhaps as significant as Achilles' regret is the epithet he gives to Odysseus: phaidim (from phaidimos). The term means "shining" or "radiant," and pronounces a god-like [daimoni isos] quality in Odysseus, who did not fight the gods but respected them.

This quality could be taken as an observation of the god-like quality of the living compared to the dead — Achilles is, after all, among the dead in this scene.

But we see similar transformations that elevate mortals not merely above the dead, but above other mortals. Two such transformations, in fact, bookend the *Odyssey*. First, we see Telemachus transformed in the first book. The goddess Athena arrives in Ithaca disguised as an old man, speaks with Odysseus' son Telamachus, and then departs:

> off and away Athena the bright-eyed goddess flew
> like a bird in soaring flight
> but left his spirit filled with nerve and courage,
> charged with his father's memory more than ever now.
> He felt his senses quicken, overwhelmed with wonder–
> this was a god, he knew it well and made at once
> for the suitors, a man like a god [*isotheos*] himself.

This god-like transformation of Telemachus is not a prelude to death, nor is the transformation of Odysseus' father, Laertes, that we find in Book 24. After reuniting with his son Odysseus, the disheveled and ragged old man takes a bath and emerges an entirely different person:

Before they ate, the Sicilian serving-woman
bathed her master, Laertes–his spirits high
in his own room–and rubbed him down with oil
and round his shoulders drew a fresh new cloak.
And Athena stood beside him, fleshing out the limbs
of the old commander, made him taller to all eyes,
His build more massive, stepping from his bath,
so his own son gazed at him, wonderstruck–
Face-to-face he seemed a deathless god [àthanátoisi theois ènalí-
gkion]...
"Father" –Odysseus' words had wings–"surely
one of the everlasting gods has made you
taller, stronger, shining in my eyes!"

For both Telemachus and Laertes, this god-like transformation is brought about by connection with Odysseus, not by antagonizing the gods so as to become glorious martyrs, as seen throughout the *Iliad*. Similarly, Achilles' address of "shining" Odysseus comes just after Odysseus has reconnected with his dead mother. In each case, these mental connections are facilitated, usually by the goddess Athena.

What we see then is a kind of solar path of theosis, one that begins by respecting the cattle of the sun, rather than taking arms against the gods. This deferential respect for the gods and the god-like protects the man from the wrath of Sun, and also leads to a mental connection. This is simultaneously a connection with the respected higher powers and a connection with others, which the gods facilitate.

This solar theosis can itself be thought of as a kind of idealism, for the connections which exist in the mind are not exactly "real" in the physical sense — and yet they exist in the world of the living. Though these connections sometimes incorporate the glorious dead, solar idealism is not limited to the dead like the idealism of the hero because it does not begin with confrontation with the immortal. Rather, it begins with deference, with "due respect" for the sun and the cattle of the sun. Through this deferential respect, the man establishes mental connection; through mental connection, the man can shine like the gods who love him for his piety.

SOLAR IDEALISM TODAY

We see much of the antagonistic, heroic impulse in youth culture today, and there is no reason to assume that this tendency is unique to our time. Indeed, works from the past give us every reason to believe it was as prevalent in 1200 BC as it is now. Punk anarchists and counter-cultural hippies have probably always been with us. It is an expression of thumos, of that passionate spiritedness that seeks recognition and glory. These people will always be with us, and as Homer tells us, most of them cannot be saved:

> the recklessness of their own ways destroyed them all,
> the blind fools [nepioi], they devoured the cattle of the Sun
> And the Sungod wiped from sight the day of their return.

"Nepioi" is translated by Fagles as "fools," and Greg Nagy translates the term as "the disconnected." But the most literal translation is "children," and conveys a kind of unregulated desire that we might associate with children.
To embrace the solar idealism of Odysseus, then, appears to be a rejection of the childish impulse that drives heroic idealism. It is more mature, more circumspect, more realistic because it begins with the real world, and not with abstractions.

It would be unrealistic (even "heroic," with all the tragic connotations of that word) to try to save everyone from this thumotic desire that so often leads to self-destruction. But for today's young men with an ear for the most respected and highly praised of the past — among which Homer is supreme — there may be wisdom in perceiving this juxtaposition of the heroic and the solar approaches of theosis, and where those who pursued each found themselves. For most of the men who died on the fields of Troy, glory was not achieved, and was not worth it to those who were glorified. But for the more mature man who did not "fight the power" and the Gods themselves, but respected them, glorification and theosis became possible, despite becoming "no man."

In today's world, such a solar path might begin by recognizing and respecting the power of existing institutions.

In theory, when these institutions deviate from their source — from a "higher god," — then they lose their legitimacy and take what is not theirs. The principle of solar deference may call for fasting from the ill-gotten harvest of illegitimate credence, because the grounding principle of legitimacy is a greater, brighter, more powerful god than the institution.

But the story of Odysseus does not call on young men to go looking for these deviations, and jumping into the ring with one's name blazoned high on a "death-or-glory" war-banner. The solar character of Odysseus is one of overt deference, even to those unworthy of such respect. In the case of the suitors, this anticipates and facilitates their massacre; in the case of disguised Athena, it earns greater aid and avoids offending a powerful Olympian god.

In a similar manner, Iliadic heroism fuels an impulse to oppose and antagonize great powers. These powers may be deemed false or malicious, but are nevertheless acknowledged as powerful. By opposing them, the naive young hero does not end them. But he may end himself.

The solar path is more strategic whether dealing with friends or foes, and especially in circumstances of ambiguity.

The path of solar deference stands apart from the heroic path in the spiritual domain as well. The hero approaches the gods as equals. Like Phaethon or Icarus falling from the sky, he is struck down for his hubris — this is his goal and perhaps a worthwhile sacrifice. But the hero who sees the high gods as equals has no room for improvement or transformation. He is only what he has been made, and is therefore guided by fate, as are all the Iliadic heroes. Brilliant Achilles is godlike because of forces beyond his control.

Shining Odysseus radiates because deference guides his eyes upward, and connection with greatness brings greatness. Whereas heroism reveals greatness among demi-gods, solar spirituality creates greatness in mortals with no divine lineage. Solar deference creates men who shine like the sun in their excellence, connected as they are with the greatness that they respect.

But to accomplish such a transformative connection, one must abstain from the hubris of taking what belongs to the gods, and from devouring the cattle of the sun.

THE APACHE STRIKER
KILLER OF ENEMIES, SON OF THE SUN
JACK DONOVAN

In *Fire in the Dark*, I remarked that while most of the examples of the Father, Striker, and Lord of the Earth god-archetypes I referred to were of Indo-European origin, I believed there were relevant analogs in many other cultures.

Men on Earth have lived under the same sky and sun and encountered many of the same challenges. They have inhabited approximately the same bodies and have seen the world through similar eyes. It makes sense, then, that they would come to many of the same conclusions independently and idealize the perfected forms of themselves in similar ways — with allowance for creativity and local color.

In evolutionary theory, the concepts of convergent evolution and recurrent evolution both fit loosely. In convergent evolution, different species independently develop characteristics not present in their shared predecessors. The independent evolution of flight in unrelated species is an example often given to explain the concept of recurrent evolution. The social institution of marriage is a recurrent or convergent cultural phenomenon. Groups of people all over the world have developed the institution of marriage independently — largely, I believe, as a solution to the problem of paternity certainty.

In much the same way, men, who have been charged always and everywhere with protecting and expanding mandalas of order in chaotic environments, seem to have evolved similar idealized versions of themselves in that role. The warrior god-archetype that I refer to as The Striker is prominent in many mythologies, and he is often associated with the sun, the sky, lightning, thunder, and birds of prey.

This month, in The Order of Fire, we've been independently studying Native American tribal mythologies, and I came across a remarkable representation of The Striker god-archetype in Apache stories about their culture hero, "Killer-of-Enemies," or "Naiyenezgani." Killer-of-Enemies is a monster slayer whose father is the Sun, and in at least one story, he carries a bow that shoots bolts of lightning.

The word Apache describes several related tribal sub-groups whose stories and practices vary substantially from group to group. The information I'm presenting here is limited to what I could find from legitimate source material from the Jicarilla, Chiricahua, Lipan, and White Mountain Apaches native to Arizona and New Mexico, where their contemporary descendants still reside. I discovered some of the same themes in the descriptions of the beliefs of the Mescalero Apache on their website.

THE BIRTH OF KILLER-OF-ENEMIES

The most detailed account of Killer-of-Enemies' birth comes from the Jicarilla Apaches, whose stories were recorded and published in the 1930s by anthropologist Morris Edward Opler.

The world creation stories of the Apaches vary considerably, but of particular note is the opening line recorded by Opler.

> "In the beginning, nothing was here where the world now stands; there was no ground, no earth,—nothing but Darkness,

Water, and Cyclone." (Opler, 1932)

This beginning from darkness or water seems almost universal mythologically, and it is tempting to link the concept of "cyclone" to "chaos." However, while in these stories, Cyclone interestingly quarrels with the lightly personified forces of Lightning and Thunder, Cyclone is occasionally benevolent and helpful toward the hero Killer-of-Enemies.

There were supernatural, god-like beings known as the Hactcin, whose existence preceded creation. As they created the material world, "They made Earth in the form of a living woman and called her Mother. They made sky in the form of a man and called him Father. He faces downward, and the woman faces up. He is our father and the woman is our mother." (Opler, 1932) So here, too, the sky is the firmament and associated with the Father. The sun and moon are created in different stories as natural phenomena but eventually become personified.

For the Jicarilla, the story of Killer-of-Enemies began when two girls wandered away from their group and up into the mountains, where they lived on fruit. When one of the girls was sleeping, the Sun turned into a man who appeared on Earth and had sex with her. On the same night, Water also turned into a man, visited the other girl, and had sex with her.

The girl who slept with the Sun became known as White-Painted Woman, and after four days, she gave birth to a boy who would become Killer-of-Enemies. The girl who slept with Water became White-Shell Woman, and after four days, she gave birth to Child-of-the-Water.

According to the White Mountain Apache version of the story, a maiden went "to the top of a high mountain and came where the rays of the rising Sun first strike. She raised her skirt and the "breath" of the Sun entered her." (Goddard, 1919) Four days later, she gave birth to Naiyenezgani, the word for "Killer or Slayer of Enemies or

Monsters." In this story, the same woman follows a similar process to create Tobatc'istcini (standardized as Tobadzischini), which roughly means "Child-of-Water." The birth process for the two heroes seems to have been similar in the Chiricahua stories. According to the Lipan Apache account, Killer-of-Enemies is associated with the sun but is the child of Thunder because his mother was impregnated by rainwater, and he combines the characteristics of Killer-of-Enemies and Child-of-Water (Opler, 1940.)

JOURNEY TO THE SOLAR FATHER

In the Jicarilla telling, Killer-of-Enemies and Child-of-Water grew older in a few days and began asking their mothers on the mountain for toys. Their mothers tell them to go east to see their fathers — though they both go to see the Sun.

On their way to see the Sun, the boys encounter various physical challenges and elemental forces like Big Rain-Storm, Lightning, Mud, Big Hail, and Snake. In most cases, the boys offered pollen and prayers to the forces they encountered and were allowed to proceed. Finally, when they reach the House of the Sun, they meet the Sun's wife. As they claimed to be the Sun's offspring, the Sun's wife became jealous, and this is identified as the birth of jealousy.

"She went inside to the sun. She said, 'I thought you said you go to the west for a good purpose and never visit other women. You have lied to me. Here are two boys who say you are their father.'" (Opler, 1932)

There's a parallel here with Hera's jealousy in the Greek lore, and her desire to torment and work against Zeus' illegitimate children — most notably, Heracles.

Before admitting that he has fathered children on his travels, the Sun puts the boys through four ordeals — ice, fire, boiling water, and the heat of the Sun. The boys survived these tests because of their supernatural lineage, so the Sun accepted them as his own.

Because Killer-of-Enemies and Child-of-Water traveled there for toys, the Sun took a hoop ring from around himself and gave the children the hoop and pole game.

The Sun remembered that there were great monsters surrounding the boys' homeland, so he gave each of them a bow made of a rainbow, arrows made of lightning, and a quiver and bow carrier made of mountain lion skin.

SLAYING CHAOS MONSTERS

As the story progresses, the teller reveals that Sun and Water impregnated the women to create heroes to save the people from the wild monsters that threatened them.

The first monster mentioned is a minotaur-like creature born when a woman "abused herself" with an elk horn. She gave birth to a giant, evil elk who could "transfix the people with his eyes and they couldn't run away when he looked at them. So they would stand immovable, and he would come up and kill them. (Opler, 1932)

Like Hercules completing his labors, while he has great power, Killer-of-Enemies also used ingenuity to kill his opponents. He hatched an elaborate plot with a gopher to dig an underground tunnel to place him beneath the heart of the Elk.

Before he started down the tunnel, Killer-of-Enemies, "asked Thunder for power, for Lightning was his arrow." (Opler, 1932)

After killing the monster elk, Killer-of-Enemies killed some giant eagles that were snatching up full-grown men and feeding on them.

He then deals with He-Kicks-them-in-the-Water, a man who sits by a narrow pass on a mountain road and kicks passersby into the boiling water below. This part of the story is almost identical to one of the six labors of Theseus, in which the robber Sciron forces people to wash his feet beside a cliff and then kicks them off to die on the rocks below or be eaten by a giant tortoise. Killer-of-Enemies and Theseus both gave this monster a taste of his own medicine and threw him off the same cliff where he had murdered others.

Killer-of-Enemies later enlisted the power of the sun to travel "at the speed of light," among other strategies, to defeat some killer rocks that were propelled by mountain sheep.

To complete the slaying of the monsters that threaten the people, Killer-of-Enemies defeated a giant owl and a giant fish — the leader of the monsters.

After slaying the monsters, Killer-of-Enemies was attacked by sorcerers. The "sorcerers tried to "shoot" him, but their "arrows" merely fell down. And the "arrows" all came back to the sorcerers, and they themselves died. That is what Killer-of-Enemies was here for, to protect the people." (Opler, 1932)

Killer-of-Enemies eventually left the people after ascending from the role of the Striker to a role more in line with the Father, giving laws and instructions about rituals. It was also suggested that he gave people free will.

"Until Killer-of-Enemies was ready to leave man, man was not living as he does now. All was as though in a dream.190 If the people had been as they are now they would have been frightened and would have run back into the hole of emergence. But when all the monsters were killed and all was at peace, Killer-of-Enemies gave people their own minds and habits, and they began to live as they do now." (Opler, 1932)

However, the storyteller also noted that after Killer-of-Enemies left, "evil and sorcery came into the lives of men."

CHIRICAHUA AND LIPAN VARIATIONS

In the stories Opler recorded from the Chiricahua Apaches, Killer-of-Enemies and Child-of-Water had similar adventures, but Killer-of-Enemies was always afraid, and Child-of-Water was the more heroic character.

In the Lipan Apache stories, the teller explains that "Killer-of-Enemies and Child-of-the-Water are two names for the same boy; there was only one boy with these two names." (Opler, 1940)
This combined character, identified primarily as Killer-of-Enemies, encounters and defeats a monstrous buffalo and an antelope. In this telling, the emphasis is on the Killer-of-Enemies transforming a giant monster who murdered people into a normal-sized version of the species that will serve as a resource for the people. He also defeated giant murdering eagles, reprimanded them, and told them to give the people their feathers for ceremonies.

As in the Jicarilla stories, Killer-of-Enemies also takes on the role of lawgiver and even creator — creating deer and horses. Killer-of-Enemies taught the people raiding and warfare, and arrow-making. When he had finished doing this and dealing with the enemies of the people, he returned home and told his mother what he had done.

"He told her his work was finished. He told her, "The new generation of people is coming. They must do all that I have done. They must follow my way and my rules."

THE WHITE MOUNTAIN APACHE STORY

In the White Mountain Apache telling, Killer-of-Enemies and Child-of-Water were conceived as described above, but were born with slight deformities. When the boys were old enough to run around and intelligent enough to ask questions, they asked about their father, and their mother reluctantly sent them on a journey to see the Sun. In this story, they rode to the Sun on the backs of a Raven and, later, an eagle — feeding both birds bits of meat they had been given to sustain them on the adventure.

When they arrived at the Sun's house, they were greeted by the Sun's jealous wife, as in the Jicarilla story. The Sun tested them by pushing them into a blazing hot place with "lightning which had sharp spines." They survived, and the Sun accepted them as his own. A sweat lodge and bath was prepared, and the sun re-shaped the boys, fixing their deformities so that they looked like men. Then the Sun gave them their names, Naiyenezgani and Tobatc'istcini. The young men then convinced the Sun to provide them with horses to ride down to the Earth. The Sun told them that there were evil things in the world and that they should kill them. He gave Killer-of-Enemies a blue sword and Child-of-Water a bow and arrow. The Sun's wife gave Killer-of-Enemies a spotted belt with a yellow fringe border.

After returning to the world, Naiyenezgani and Tobatc'istcini encountered a blind man with eyes in the back of his head who was killing people — an enemy (Naiye') — and they killed him.

THE APACHE STRIKER

The Striker god-archetype is the warrior beyond warriors who contends with physical chaos, creating and expanding the perimeter of order. He is the lightning and the storm of heaven who does the dirty, wet work of the more distant, ascended Father in the sky. While men have worshiped gods, our best Striker stories are often about heroic demi-gods — who are perhaps more relatable than deathless superhuman entities.

Achilles, Herakles, Gilgamesh, Perseus, and Cú Chulainn were all half-sons of gods or goddesses. Herakles and Perseus were both sons of Zeus, who descended upon mortal women who were then forced to rear their partially divine sons on Earth — like the Kents raising Superman. These heroic demi-gods are of the people, at once salt-of-the-earth and spawn of the sky. It's easy to imagine the hero who does what no other man can or will do as having some otherworldly origin — some magical fated blood from beyond that makes him special.

Killer-of-Enemies matches the well-established form of a people's hero of supernatural origin. He's the son of the Sun, created intentionally to do battle against monsters, murderers, and enemies of humanity on behalf of a benevolent god. Strikers tend to be associated with storms and lightning, from Indra and Zeus to Thor, so the fact that in one telling, the Sun gives him arrows of lightning is another alignment with our Striker. In another telling, he defeats his enemies, like the monstrous buffalo and antelope, into resources for the people — recalling Indra slaying the dragon Vrtra to release the waters of the world.

One standout feature of the Killer-of-Enemies story is that he is usually accompanied by a more earthly counterpart, Child-of-Water, who we might link loosely to a character like Enkidu in the Gilgamesh story, who is also a man of the earth than the sky.

Another distinct feature of Naiyenezgani's story is that he is a boy for most of it. In the Jicarilla story of his adventure at the owl's home, not recounted here, he learns not to disobey the Sun by narrowly escaping death at the hands of a murderous giant owl. (Opler, 1932) As many of the other Apache stories that have come down to us explain simple things about the world, warn children not to disobey, and warn about the dangers of self-abuse and early sex or elaborately explain the purpose of puberty rites — it seems that the primary function of these stories is to educate and inspire children. The stories about Killer-of-Enemies are meant to inspire courage and heroism in boys and young men and initiate them into their roles as protectors and benefactors of the people who may be called on to slay murderers and enemies, as well as dangerous wild beasts who "give themselves" to the people for clothing and sustenance.

Killer-of-Enemies is another reflection and mythic idealization of the man-as-warrior that we can comfortably add to our collection of known Strikers. Each of these myths from around the world can teach us something different about the nature of men and what it means to be an exemplary man who is good at being a man. Each representation of this eternal ideal can add new depth and a new aesthetic dimension to our holistic understanding of men and masculinity and to our understanding and perception of ourselves.

SOURCES

Goddard,Pliny Earle. *Myths and Tales from the White Mountain Apache*. First published in Anthropological Papers of the American Museum of Natural History, Vol. XXIV, Part II, by Order of the Trustees, New York, 1919. Owlfoot Press. Kindle Edition.

Opler, Edward Morris. *Myths and Tales of the Jicarilla Apache Indians (Native American)*. Dover Publications. Originally Published 1932. Kindle Edition.

Opler, Morris Edward. *Myths and Legends of the Lipan Apache Indians*. Originally Published 1940. Borodino Books. Kindle Edition.

Opler, Morris Edward; French, David H.. *Myths and Tales of the Chiricahua Apache Indians*. Originally Published 1942. Borodino Books. Kindle Edition.

Uncited Source

Goddard, Pliny Earle. *Jicarilla Apache Texts*. First published 1911. Pantianos Classics.

THE AIM OF AGENCY
SHOOTING AS AN ORIGIN OF CONSCIOUSNESS
C.B. ROBERTSON AND ED HAMANN

"You have become a different person in the course of these years. For this is what the art of archery means: a profound and far–reaching contest of the archer with himself. Perhaps you have hardly noticed it yet, but you will feel it very strongly when you meet your friends and acquaintances again in your own country: things will no longer harmonize as before. You will see with other eyes and measure with other measures. It has happened to me too, and it happens to all who are touched by the spirit of this art."

— Eugene Herrigal, *Zen and the Art of Archery*, 1953

HOMO SAPIENS: THE SHOOTING HOMINID

We've all heard stories about "amazing shots." Usually these stories star sharpshooters, on screen or on the battlefield, calmly and precisely taking down a target at a seemingly impossible distance. This might be Quigley, hitting a bucket while standing at 782 yards. Or Chris Kyle killing an enemy sniper at 2100 yards. Something about these stories captivates us, and we tell them over and over again, with different men behind the trigger – not just John Russel, Bob Lee Swagger, and the Gunslinger, but back to Robin Hood, splitting an arrow. Or Odysseus, threading the axe-heads with his heavy bow.

Hitting the target at a distance is an act of primordial importance, to the point of species-defining. Our gifts that helped us thrive in the distant past were extraordinary endurance (surpassing even wolves and horses), an immensely complex vocal range which permitted more precise communication, and the ability to hit things from a distance with force and accuracy – initially by throwing, and later by launching with bows and guns.

Combined, these three skills – endurance, communication, and launching projectiles — made humans the deadliest predators on the planet.

Today, nothing *stops* us from developing our endurance, even if this once universal virtue is no longer as evenly distributed as it once was.

Endurance seems to have simultaneously increased and decreased. The average American will get winded by a couple flights of stairs, and yet a significant minority have taken up running as a habit. Some have taken endurance to unfathomable extremes, like running the infamous 135 mile "Badwater Ultramarathon" through Death Valley. In July.

Meanwhile, linguistic skill might be at historical peaks. More jobs require broader communication skills with more people than ever before. Most of us go to school for longer than even the most educated of the past, where we are taught writing and speaking in a more or less formal system.

But things are different with shooting. The violent nature of shooting has always caused fearful people to seek prohibitions against others possessing ranged weapons. Most Western nations today ban or seriously restrict many types of firearms, and even some bows (like crossbows).

For this reason, if there is something significantly human about shooting, it is in greater need of articulation and defense than speech or running.

And there is something significantly human about shooting. Aside from its primitive role in hunting and combat, there is evidence that the act of shooting was critical in the development of human agency and consciousness. If this is true, then the loss of shooting — an aim often advanced by anxious safety advocates — risks not only a loss of connection with our past, but also with a deeper part of ourselves.

THE PHENOMENOLOGY OF SHOOTING

On paper, shooting is a relatively simple act. We raise our tool — perhaps a bow, perhaps a gun— and sight down our target. We release the string or pull the trigger. We feel the instrument act, and then after some brief time interval, we see the hit or miss on our target.

But more is going on in the act than meets the eye.

Here, we must take a moment to first distinguish between shooting and its far more ancient cousin: throwing.

When walking through the woods, we may decide to throw a rock at a nearby object — perhaps a squirrel, or the hornet-nest next to our friend. The rock that we pick up is of uneven shape and unknown weight. We go by instinct, lobbing it as best we can with the arms nature gave us.

Suppose we missed — "unlucky," we say to ourselves. It had to be a judgment call; we did not know the weight or shape of the rock in advance, having to judge how it would fly by feel. An easy thing to miscalculate.

But suppose we decide to return to camp and get better. We collect five stones of near-identical shape and weight. We practice, and our skill with one rock transfers to skill with the other rocks. We come to understand them. We figure out roughly where we have to aim to hit at different distances, and make our throw more consistent in power with practice. With this systematization, we have — imperceptibly, but significantly — moved forward from merely throwing. What started as a desire to hit an object at a distance has begun to evolve into a system for hitting harder, from further away, and with greater precision. A sling permits tremendously increased power with a stone. A spear gives us a throwing missile, more damaging than a mere rock, and a tool like an atlatl provides power to the spear in the way a sling gives more power to a stone throw.

But with a bow-string — which, when drawn to the same spot on the cheek, will release the same arrow at the same speed every time — we achieve an ability to hone our aim with power and precision mechanically unlike previous advancements. It is with the bow, perhaps, that we achieve "shooting."

Shooting is not instinctive in the same way as throwing. While "instinctive shooting" is certainly a style and approach that even modern archers still use, there is a difference in the equipment. Whether it is a stick bow or a precision rifle, the technology involved with shooting reduces variation. In other words, the shooter becomes responsible for the success or failure of the shot in a way that is controllable, in proportion to the precision of his tools.

Of course, the stone-thrower is also mechanically responsible for his hits and misses, but it is felt differently with shooting. Responsibility is something the shooter experiences *as agency*. The archer releases a bit early, and long before the arrow hits its target, he knows it will be short. A shooter anticipates the recoil of his pistol and pushes down before pulling the trigger. If he is experienced, he will recognize the movement and realize his fault. The understanding of failure is possible precisely because of the reliability of the system, which we don't see with slings and tomahawks.

Indeed, the earliest forms of agency must have taken baby-steps in the smallest possible increments of time in experiencing one's own actions as causes.

On this ground alone, shooting provides a setting which could explain how the experience of agency once arose in our species. Throwing may have laid the groundwork, but the systematized nature of shooting also provides an *incentive* for agency, in a way that other activities do not. Those with higher agency and a greater sense of personal action will be more likely to hit over time, because when they miss, they are more likely to blame themselves than a God or some other force. They experience themselves as a cause, and not merely as a conduit.

Explaining the origin of agency would, by necessity, also explain the rise of consciousness. Agency is a subset of consciousness; without consciousness, we would be like wolves or sharks, relying upon instinct and natural intelligence to hunt and survive.

When we speak of consciousness, we are speaking both of subjective sensation generally — why is it "like" anything to exist — and also of our awareness of this sensation — the experience of being "you," which is sometimes called "self-consciousness." When philosophers speak of the "hard problem of consciousness", they are speaking of the former. This question is a metaphysical mystery. This basic sense may not be unique to humans; as philosopher Thomas Nagel famously argued, it is almost certainly "like" something to be a bat, whether we can see any evidence of that subjective experience or not.

What distinguishes humans and interests us here is the latter, self-aware sense of consciousness. This is both our recognition of ourselves in the mirror, and our sense of agency in the world around us — that we can choose to make things happen.

Without this, we could very well go through life on instinct, and even having "thoughts." Psychologist Julian Jaynes described the hypothetical pre-conscious man as a man living in a world of gods and spirits, where his own thoughts would arrive to him as if through the voice of an external source. With animals, we can recognize that they have a subjective experience, but lack this sense of agency — when owners punish their dogs, the dog does not have the same understanding of *why* they are being punished that we do. What we perceive as "guilt" is a projection of our own, and nothing more than the animals' foreboding that they are about to be punished for something (and over time, they will "learn" what not to do by unconscious association).

This experience of self-hood is by no means purely positive. Consciousness brings with it the possibilities of anxiety, despair, and self-pity. By itself, consciousness is taxing, and without a fruitful object of attention, self-awareness can be completely debilitating. Consciousness is justified if it is accompanied by some sense of "agency" — the experience of being a cause in our surroundings. With agency, consciousness is a tool of perception across time that permits us to act, build, create, and strike, in manners we could never have imagined as unconscious creatures. Without agency, consciousness only carries its costly, paralytic downsides.

We might consider for evidence our current generation of adolescents and young adults, who have been made hyper-aware of their own identity and consciousness — perhaps in relation to any number of quickly multiplying causes that activists are persistently trying to "raise awareness" about. This population suffers some of the worst mental health in recorded history, with prescription medications for anxiety and depression that may not be sufficient to deal with the "heightened consciousness" we have managed to achieve of things we can do nothing about.

But with the immense power of shooting, the reward for consciousness might have begun to outweigh the costs.

It may be beyond our ability to prove where consciousness came from — let alone shooting as a specific origin. But the connection between shooting and consciousness in our experience and in our language and stories should make the hypothesis at least plausible. But perhaps more importantly, it establishes the connection: regardless of origin, shooting has always been connected metaphorically to consciousness, and we can see this in our myths and very language.

MORALITY VERSUS VIRTUE – SHOOTING AS THE ORIGIN OF "SIN"

There is a kind of moral judgment inherent in the experience of shooting. The success or failure of a shot rests upon the shooter because systematization accounts for everything else. He is praiseworthy if he hits, and blameworthy if he misses. A man might be attractive for his gifts, like his height, natural strength, or inborn intelligence. These positive qualities are "virtues," or "excellences," and are respected as valuable whether he is responsible for them or not. Throwing might be considered among these kinds of virtue. We don't hold it against men *morally* for lacking certain gifts, even if we maintain a preference for virtuous company.

Morality is different from virtue. To be moral implies agency and an ability to have done otherwise. To judge someone morally is to judge their actions and their choice, not their nature, and to distinguish their actions *from* their nature. To judge others morally is to ascribe agency to them. To judge ourselves morally is to ascribe agency to ourselves, and to experience that agency in our own judgment. Virtue can be possessed by unconscious men, and even detected unconsciously, while morality requires consciousness.

Wouldn't it be interesting if our earliest moral language — as distinct from virtue language — corresponds with shooting?

Indeed, this is exactly what we find, and in disparate cultures too. One of the key words that distinguishes morality from virtue has its etymological origins in shooting.

In the religious history of the West, our use of the word "sin" has etymological roots in Proto-Germanic *sundiō*, or perhaps Old Norse sannr, or Latin sons; all variously translate as "guilty." But "sin" came into common use as a translation from Christian texts, which used the Hebrew ḥāṭā' (חטא) and Greek hamartía (ἁμαρτία) as their foundation. The words mean "to miss" and "to miss the mark," respectively. We find the same etymology in the root for "sin" in the Sanskrit aparādh (अपराध). Colloquially understood, it means to offend, wrong, or sin, but literally translates as missing the mark.

To the ancients, the very idea of "sin," with all of its cosmic and spiritual significance, was best understood and articulated in reference to our ability to hit a target. The sinful man is the man who — due to some moral flaw, and not merely a deficiency in virtue — failed in the act of shooting.

There is reason to suspect Greek and Sanskrit may have shared a common root in the Proto-Indo-European language family. But Hebrew comes from a different linguistic group, meaning there are possibly two independent linguistic origins for the same concept of "sin," as a moral failing, expressed through the language of archery. To the degree that shooting formed the origins of consciousness and agency, this language would not have been metaphorical but literal, and the experience of moral failing would have been felt first in the activity of shooting, and only then extended outward into other domains of human life.

Beyond the words for sin, we find a connection between consciousness and shooting in ancient myths: namely in the characters of Rama, Arjuna, Odysseus, and Apollo.

Archery also holds an important status in the great epics of the Indian subcontinent. To fight with a bow and arrow is traditionally considered most excellent and is the weapon of choice for two of the most important figures in Hindu mythology. The first is the warrior-prince Rama, the principal figure of the Ramayana, and the second is Arjuna, a main protagonist of the Mahabharata and the primary figure of its well-known portion known as Bhagavad Gita.

RAMA

The most famous incident involving Rama and a bow takes place in the first chapter of the Ramayana and details the winning of his bride, Sita. Janaka, the king of Videha, was plowing a field in preparation for a fire sacrifice and a girl sprang up from behind his plow.

> Now, once as I was ploughing a field, a girl sprang up from behind my plough. I found her as I was clearing the field, and she is thus known by the name Sita 'Furrow'. Sprung from the earth, she has been raised as my daughter, and, since she was not born from the womb, my daughter has been set apart as one for whom the only bride-price is strength. (Goldman and Goldman page 118)

The test would be the stringing of the god Shiva's bow, a family heirloom kept in an eight-wheeled iron chest said to require five thousand men to haul. Many kings asked for the hand of Sita but none could even grasp the bow, let alone lift it or string it. Janaka saw them as weak and refused to allow any of them to marry Sita. The kings became angry believing their failures would bring them disrepute and laid siege on the capital for a year, exhausting the resources of the kingdom. King Janaka did penance and was given a large army from the gods to drive away the suitors. They were routed in retreat while being slaughtered.

One day the great sage Vishvamitra, along with Rama, and his brother Lakshman, came to visit King Janaka. There was an offer to show the bow to Rama.

> Rama opened the chest in which the bow lay and regarding it closely, he then spoke: "Now brahman, I shall touch this great bow with my hand. I shall attempt to lift and even to string it." "Very well," replied both the king and the sage. So, following the sage's instructions, he easily grasped the bow in the middle. Then, as though it were mere play to him, the righteous prince,

the delight of the Raghus, strung the bow as thousands watched. The mighty man affixed the bowstring and, nocking an arrow to it, drew it back. But in doing so, the best of men broke the bow in the middle. (Goldman and Goldman page 119)

The text describes a thundering noise and trembling of the earth at the breaking of the bow that causes everyone in attendance to fall except the king, the sage, Rama, and his brother. With the bride-price fulfilled, Janaka joyfully offers Sita in marriage.

The bow is not only a symbol of Rama's great strength; it is a symbol of his morality, virtue, and divine origin. A divine origin as the seventh incarnation (*avatār*) of Lord Vishnu — the source of absolute consciousness and therefore agency. The inability of the suitor kings to string the bow and their subsequent behavior shows their lack of morality — a wickedness (*paap karna*).

It is noteworthy that in this story, moral goodness — and the agency that distinguishes morality from mere excellence — is a requirement to even lift the bow, which has become magnified into enormous proportions. This symbolic transfer unites morality with the act of shooting, and perhaps transforms shooting into a metaphor for action itself, just as "missing the mark" became an expression describing moral failure in general.

ARJUNA

Arjuna was known as the greatest of all warriors and archers yet a pivotal moment involving the bow for him is in stark contrast to the previously detailed story from the *Ramayana*.

The Kurukshetra war is the central battle that takes place within the epic poem the *Mahabharata*. The war is the result of a struggle for succession between two groups of cousins of the Kuru Dynasty, the Pandavas and the Kauravas. As the two armies gather, the Pandava prince Arjuna asks his charioteer, Krishna, to take him to the center of the battlefield to observe the assembled armies. He sees among them his own relatives, respected teachers, and friends. He becomes filled with doubt at the prospect of killing them and contemplates leaving the battlefield.

He turns to Krishna and pleads with him to tell him what is the right thing to do. The discourse that takes place between Krishna and Arjuna is known as the *Bhagavad Gita* (or "Song of God").

Chapter 1 of the Gita is often referred to as Arjuna Vishada Yoga (the yoga of Arjuna's sorrow). The language in Verse 46 describes Arjuna's anguish as *śoka-saṃvigna-mānasaḥ* — his mind "distracted and agitated by sorrow." Arjuna rationalizes that his desire not to cause harm is a moral-duty that shows discretion and compassion. He goes so far as to say it would be better if he himself were to be killed unarmed on the battlefield. He throws aside his bow and arrows and sits down on the chariot, engulfed in grief.

Krishna admonishes Arjuna not to give in to impotence. He tells him that his state of mind is not true compassion or discretion, but *kṣudram hṛdaya-daurbalyam* — "petty lamentation and delusion." Weakness at such a crucial time does not befit his status as a *kshatriya*, a member of the warrior class. It will neither enhance his reputation nor lead to the heavenly planets. It will lead to infamy. Krishna urges him to arise and do battle. He has a choice, and putting down the bow and choosing not to fight would be immoral — the epitome of sin.

The battlefield of Kurukshetra is also known as Dharmakshetra (the field of duty), which means the mythic landscape of the *Bhagavad Gita* paints taking up the bow as the central representation of moral duty. The fulfillment of Arjuna's duty (*dharma*) rests in his ability to shoot with one-pointed consciousness (*ekāgratā*), in full absorption and undisturbed attention.

ODYSSEUS

The *Iliad* is a book of fate, framed at its very outset with the idea that "the will of Zeus was moving toward its end." By contrast, the *Odyssey* is a book of agency, and Homer describes even the Gods (including fate-sealing Zeus) ascribing agency to mortals below:

"Ah how shameless–the way these mortals blame the gods.

From us alone, they say, come all their miseries, yes,

But they themselves, with their own reckless ways,

Compound their pains beyond their proper share..."

In the *Odyssey*, consciousness is Odysseus' superpower. He is the man of mind, or consciousness, of nous. In the opening, theme-setting lines of the book, it is said that he saw "many cities of men [...] and learned to know their minds (*nous*)." In juxtaposition with the glory (*kleos*) of Achilles, Odysseus stands as a kind of narrative embodiment and symbol of consciousness in the world of Homer.

This consciousness is ultimately manifested in the famous scene in the dining hall of Ithaca. Penelope has laid out a challenge for the suitors, with the promise that she will marry the winner — the challenge being to string her husband's bow and shoot through a series of axe-heads. After all the suitors failed to even string the Odysseus' great bow, Odysseus — disguised as an old man — strings the bow with ease and shoots through the axe-heads, before turning and dispatching the suitors with the same weapon. The suitors' failure to recognize the true king is thematically indicative of their unconsciousness. Like Odysseus' comrades who could not be saved because of their recklessness, they are nepioi — literally "children," sometimes translated as "disconnected" or "fools." Their failure to utilize the bow represents "sin" and moral failure of character.

Again, it is the bow which is associated with moral excellence or sin.

APOLLO

Elsewhere in the Hellenic world, we can see this connection between morality, consciousness, and shooting in the gods themselves — in one god in particular.

Apollo, he who "shoots from afar," is also the god of morality. It is the moral failings of Agamemnon in relation to Apollo that begins the drama of the story of the *Iliad*, and it is Apollo who punishes the hubris of Agamemnon, "arrows for tears." While other deities like Zeus dictate certain customs of hospitality, and Athena of civic relations, it is Apollo who enjoins his followers to a decidedly internal ethic — "morality" as distinct from "virtue." It is only through this conscious self-perception that virtues such as "moderation" and "self-knowledge" become possible as moral virtues:

This apotheosis of individuation, if it be at all conceived as imperative and laying down precepts, knows but one law—the individual, i.e., the observance of the boundaries of the individual, measure in the Hellenic sense. Apollo, as ethical deity, demands due proportion of his disciples, and, that this may be observed, he demands self-knowledge. And thus, parallel to the æsthetic necessity for beauty, there run the demands "know thyself" and "not too much"...

Apollo is many things, but he is not all things. His joining of archery and the morality of consciousness is a unique connection among that wide-ranging pantheon of complex deities, not merely chance. His very character evokes — in golden, solar imagery — the origins of consciousness and morality itself in the Striker, in the one who shoots from afar.

SHOOTING AND CONSCIOUSNESS

On the etymological, mythical, and phenomenological evidence, there is reason to believe that shooting gave birth to agency and its twin, consciousness; that consciousness in turn gave birth to morality, as distinct from virtue, and together, these changes reshaped and enshrined themselves in the language and myth of humanity, wrapping themselves in the characters and even the very words of the technical means that created them.

This hypothesis seems more plausible than consciousness emerging from mere complexity, or arising out of the collapse of bicameralism.

But regardless of where consciousness arose from, these stories and words – as well as our own experience – show a profound connection between shooting and consciousness, one that can tell us much about ourselves, both in the past and the present. Our abilities as endurance animals and speakers are important and species-defining, and a connection with these is usually understood to be important both for our physical and psychological health. Perhaps there is a spiritual dimension too, in terms of connecting with our primordial ancestors and the highest skills we have inherited from nature. But these stories show that shooting is important as well, to a similar degree as speech or running. Shooting is fundamental to our humanity, more so even than consciousness itself.

APOLLO'S BROKEN MASK
REMEMBER WHY YOU STARTED
JACK DONOVAN

In 1994, the infamous tomb robber Pietro Casasanta discovered a broken ivory mask of Apollo near the remains of the Baths of Claudius, just north of Rome. The mask is believed to have been carved by Phidias in the fifth Century BCE. Phidias was the sculptor responsible for the Athene Parthenos and the statue of Zeus at Olympia, known as one of the seven wonders of the ancient world. Like those two statues, it is assumed that the "mask" was actually the face of a man-sized statue made of ivory and gold, supported by a wooden armature.

All that remains of that once proud statue of a youthful god is a scarred and chipped face discarded and found 2,500 years later in the dirt of foreign country. The mask was smuggled through an underground network of art dealers until it was seized by authorities in London and returned to Italy.

Now Apollo's weathered, disembodied face is on display in a museum.

2

Apollo was an important god to the ancient Greeks, but a compli-
cated one. He was the son of Zeus and a Striker like him, known
for slaying the dragon Python at Delphi. In those mountains at
the navel of the world, marked with the egg-like omphalos stone,
Apollo became a god of truth and prophecy – revealing the mind of
his father. And, as a god of revelation, he was also a giver of light and
brightness associated with the sun. Apollo was regarded as both
a healer and a god of plague. He played the lyre and was known as
a god of music and poetry, but notably, it was his wild and earthy
brother, Dionysus, who became the god of the theater.

Nietzsche famously set Apollo and Dionysus at odds in *The Birth of
Tragedy* as a way to explain the character and creation of art. To ac-
complish this, he pushed the singing, cithara-plucking Apollo out of
the realm of music, emphasizing his connection to the visible arts
of sculpture and architecture, meanwhile reserving the mysterious,
passionate, and imageless domain of music for his wine-loving
brother.

For Nietzsche, the beautiful, moderate, and well-ordered Apollonian
world of the Greeks was a response to the chaotic sensuality and
cruelty of the natural world. Nietzsche's Apollo symbolized the
spirit of individuation – contrasted with the sense of oneness and
ego-death experienced during sex, intoxication, musical ecstasy,
extreme emotion, and the undulations of the mob.

Camille Paglia elaborated on Nietzsche's theme in *Sexual Personae*:

> "Dionysus is the empathic, the sympathetic emotion trans-
> porting us into other people, other places, other times. Apollo is
> the hard, cold separatism of western personality and categori-
> cal thought. Dionysus is energy, ecstasy, hysteria, promiscuity,
> emotionalism—heedless indiscriminateness of idea or practice.
> Apollo is obsessiveness, voyeurism, idolatry, fascism—frigidity
> and aggression of the eye, petrifaction of objects."

This stark contrast between the sons of Zeus has captured the imaginations of many. However, it is easy to lose the character of Apollo in this theory of the "Apollonian" first devised in the late 19th Century.

The ancient Greeks were a thoughtful people. But, surely, they would not have characterized themselves as having created the "Apollonian" Greek world as a response to the chthonic womb or the brutality of nature. This dialectical construction was designed to make a particular point.

There is every reason to believe that ancient Greek paganism developed as organically as the Erechtheion – constructed and reconstructed to incorporate the accumulation and evolution of myths over the centuries.

Likewise, it is reasonable to assume that Apollo's mysteriously broad and sometimes contradictory collection of talents and associations was also acquired as he traveled through space and time.

3

In primary literary sources from Homer to Aeschylus and in ancient artworks like the ivory mask, there is little trace of this cold and calculated "Apollonian" persona.

Many would do well to remember that the statuary of the ancient world was often colorfully painted. Apollo's vacant gaze would hit different if you could see the dazzling sparkle of his bejeweled or painted eyes – as the Athenians saw him.

Apollo's character in myth, epic poetry, and drama is passionate and thumotic.

In *Agamemnon*, the doomed seeress Cassandra explained her plight by telling the story of a horny Apollo who offered her the gift of prophecy and then "came like a wrestler, magnificent," took her down, and "breathed his fire" through her. When she rejected his advances at the last moment, he cursed her and told her no one would ever believe her stories.

Later in the three-part drama of the *Oresteia*, we learn that it was Apollo who told Orestes to avenge his father by killing his own mother, acting as the voice of patriarchy, and he reminded everyone that Zeus spoke through him.

In the opening lines of the *Iliad*, after Agamemnon seized the daughter of one of Apollo's priests and refused to return her, the bright god strode down "from Olympus' peaks, storming at heart with his bow and hooded quiver slung across his shoulders. The arrows clanged at his back as the god quaked with rage, the god himself on the march and down he came like night." Apollo cut down men with his plague arrows for days until the girl was finally returned to his temple.

Callimachus composed his "Hymn to Apollo" in the 3rd Century BCE and described Apollo as dressed in a golden tunic, ever beautiful and young, but also insisted that:

> "None is so abundant in skill as Apollo. To him belongs the archer, to him the minstrel; for unto Apollo is given in keeping alike archery and song. His are the lots of the diviner and his the seers; and from Phoebus do leeches know the deferring of death."

Perhaps Nietzsche was closer to the mark concerning Apollo the god when he claimed that "Homeric 'naïveté' is only to be understood as the complete triumph of the Apollonian illusion."

A cynical man – or a dragon – might call the sublime dream of Homer's heroic stories a "noble lie." He would say that it's a tale too good to be true, too perfect to be real, something so high that it is far beyond the reach of these clumsy balding monkeys.

I'd like to imagine that Apollo would reply that it was something worth reaching toward anyway – like reaching for the sun, a solar ideal.

Or perhaps – and I think this is more likely – Zeus' loyal son Apollo would dismiss all of this cleverness out of hand and return his attention to hunting dragons, heretics, and other such naysayers.

4

Apollo was one of the most prominent Olympian gods, revered throughout the Greek world and later adopted by the Romans. But Apollo was also essentially an eternal teenager – always described and depicted as a beardless youth.

In the context of comparative religion, this is somewhat strange. Young men are often heroes – Cú Chulainn comes to mind – and, naturally, boys feature prominently as protagonists in folklore and fairytales meant for children. But gods are typically men or fully grown adult creatures.

Even in our youth-obsessed consumer culture, the people who take teenagers most seriously today are the politicians and marketers who see them as easy and insecure marks. Most adults remember how foolish they were as teenagers and associate adolescence with foolishness – making exception for those sad, stunted types who "peaked" in high school and never moved on.

A teenager in ancient Greece was certainly harder and more impressive than most young men his age today – especially after years of beating his peers bloody in the palaestra. But still, why would an entire culture of warlike, intelligent men worship a teenage god?

Some will suggest that Apollo's youthful appearance is due to his association with iconic *kouros* statues and whatever they represented to the Greeks. The word kouros indicates a young man, usually of noble birth, and Apollo was sometimes referred to as the "*megistos kouros*" or "the greatest kouros." A step further into the realm of conjecture connects the *kouroi* to the **kóryos*, a reconstructed Proto-Indo-European word used to describe a roving war-band of young, unmarried youths undergoing an initiatory transition into manhood. Scholars have drawn attention to similarities in the practices of various institutionalized fraternal groups throughout Indo-European cultures and speculated that they may have been echoes of this "**kóryos*." We will never know if this is true or not. It seems likely that many of the ideas and practices associated with the **kóryos* follow naturally from the combined experiences of male adolescence and of assuming the primal role of men in a gang of hunters and fighters at the perimeters of a given society's social order.

But what is essential to our discussion of Apollo is that this connection to initiatory groups highlights the transitional period of adolescence as a period in which we begin shaping our identities as men.

Adolescence is a time of becoming. It's a time when young men are testing themselves and taking on new responsibilities – when they're learning things for the first time and, in a healthy society, listening to what older men have to say and taking it to heart. The world of men is new to them – and no matter how hard or smart they're trying to be, they're still somewhat innocent and a little bit naïve. We can laugh at that cynically, or we can recognize the value of its purity and elevate it. Elevate the magic of a confident young man trying his hardest to become something, to demonstrate his worth, to impress the accomplished men above him and to do what he has been taught is right, and to feel that rightness with passion and certainty.

That, right there. *That's* Apollo. That is a god worthy of reverence.

A god who symbolizes the youthful purity of action and intent.

5

As a man, I hope you have some memory of what that's like.

I hope you can recognize it in young men, and I hope it makes you smile because it shows that something is right in the world.

As you know, things do become more complicated. Even a good man eventually finds himself in a position of wariness and moral uncertainty, having been beguiled by less than noble lies and tangled in a relativism of too many variables and unclear outcomes.

The Greeks knew this – they *invented* tragedy and the weaving of confusing plots and tales of political machination and corruption. The Greeks...were not naïve.

But they had Apollo there, eternally youthful, shooting perfectly straight from worlds away.

Young men are animated by a purity of intent. Even grown men experience this, depending on the character of their motivations, as they begin new endeavors. We feel it when we try to learn a new skill or when we're inspired to do something because it is worth doing, or because we believe it is beautiful, or because we think the world needs it.

But in the doing of the thing and dealing with the damnable day-in and day-out of it – all of the setbacks and side-quests and even the unforeseen consequences of success – in the midst of all that... well, that initial spark, that purity gets lost and forgotten. And you look back and wonder what happened and maybe try to find that again.

So now, when I think about what Apollo may have meant to the Greeks, it might seem strange, but some Bob Seger lyrics come to mind. They're from a song about an older man, frustrated by his complicated life, remembering the purity, clarity, and energy he had as a young man.

My hands were steady, my eyes were clear and bright

My walk had purpose, my steps were quick and light

And I held firmly to what I felt was right... [1]

In the chorus, he describes his younger self in the language of Apollo – "standing arrow straight" – and in this ghostly vision, he sees himself again.

The ivory face of Apollo symbolizes the eternal incorruptibility of youth, the unwavering belief in a righteous endeavor, and the willingness to slay dragons and cut down armies for it.

If you've lost that...you may have to dig through some dirt to find it.

It may be cracked and chipped.

But it's there, waiting.

Go find it.

Pick it up and dust it off.

Hold it up.

Think about who you wanted to be.

And remember why you started.

---

[1] Seger, Bob. "Like a Rock." *Like a Rock*, Capitol Records, May 1986.

GHEE : THE HOLY OIL
ED HAMANN

Rig Veda Mandala 6 Sukta 16.11

tam tvā samidbhir aṅgiro ghṛtena vardhayāmasi | bṛhac chocā yaviṣṭhya ||

You, Angiras, with kindling sticks and with holy oil (ghee) do we strengthen.
Blaze fiercely, youngest of the Gods.

Originating in ancient India, Ghee is clarified butter that has been slowly melted to separate the milk solids from the golden butterfat on the surface then simmered until the solids settle at the bottom of the pan and begin to brown, resulting in a nutty, caramel-like flavor and aroma. It differs from French clarified butter where the butterfat is simply separated from the milky solids. Ghee is cooked until all of the water has evaporated before the pure butterfat is strained. The smoking point rises to about 375°F making it suitable for frying and sautéing and if properly stored can be kept at room temperature for months.

Ghee is to the Indian diet what olive oil is to the Mediterranean and modern nutritional research tells us that ghee is a source of beta carotene, vitamins A, D, E, and K as well as the essential fatty acid ALA (alpha linoleic acid). It is free of casein, is lactose free, and contains no oxidized cholesterol. The traditional Indian science of holisic health, called *Ayurveda*, considers ghee a *rasayana* (rejuvenative substance) that increases intelligence, intellect, memory, and internal juices of the body (*rasa*).

Ghee is also an important illumination oil. Most common now for the *arati* ceremony, the offering of lamps in temples. The light of burning ghee is said to ward off negativity and evil influence.

The bodies of deities are ritually smeared with ghee and it is an important component of *panchamrit* (five nectars)- a mixture of milk, yogurt, ghee, honey, and sugar used in their ceremonial bathing. The concoction is then considered sanctified and sipped from the palm of the hand by devtotees. Hindu mythology even tells of a sea of clarified butter called *ajyavari* आज्यवारि.

Ghee has signified wealth, prosperity, and regeneration in India for millennia and in Vedic times was compared to liquid gold. Called *ghrita* घृत in Sanskrit, it comes from the root *ghr* घृ, which means to sprinkle, wet or moisten, to drop (as in droplets) or to shine or illumine. When used as part of Vedic fire sacrifice, called *yajña* यज्ञ, it is known as *ajya* आज्य, meaning anything fit for oblation, and *havisya* हविष्य, barley or rice mixed with ghee. Vedic hymns mention special wooden ladles, called *sruc* सुच्, used for pouring ghee onto the fire. They are described as being the length of an arm with a beak-like spout.

There is a late Vedic ghee origin story involving Prajapati, lord of the creatures. He rubbed ("churned") his hands together to create the primordial ghee, which he then poured into the sacrificial flames to create his offspring. (It would seem that butter here is a symbol for semen and the rubbing or churning a representation of the sexual act.) When the Vedic ritual is performed by introducing streams of ghee into the sacred fire it is a reenactment of creation.

Mandala 4 Sukta 58 of the Rig Veda praises ghee in a rather esoteric way. It is the only hymn in the Rig Veda *dedicated solely to ghee.*

RV 4.58.1

समुद्रादूर्मिर्मधुमाँ उदारदुपांशुना सममृतत्वमानट् । घृतस्य नाम गुह्यं यदस्ति जिह्वा देवानाममृतस्य नाभिः ॥

samudrād ūrmir madhumāṁ ud ārad upāṃśunā sam amṛtatvam ānaṭ |
ghṛtasya nāma guhyaṃ yad asti jihvā devānām amṛtasya nābhiḥ ||

From the sea a honeyed wave has arisen; along with the (soma-) plant it has reached all the way to immortality.

The name of Ghee that is hidden: "the tongue of the gods," "the navel of the immortal."

RV 4.58.1

वयं नाम प्र ब्रवामा घृतस्यास्मिन्यज्ञे धारयामा नमोभिः । उप ब्रह्मा शृणवच्छस्यमानं चतुःशृङ्गोऽवमीद्गौर एतत् ॥

vayaṃ nāma pra bravāmā ghṛtasyāsmin yajñe dhārayāmā namobhiḥ | upa brahmā śṛṇavac chasyamānaṃ catuḥśṛṅgo 'vamīd gaura etat ||

We will proclaim the name of Ghee; at this sacrifice here we will uphold it with reverences.

The formulator will hear it as it is being announced. The four-horned buffalo [=soma] has vomited it.

There is some useful symbolism within myths and rituals that attach a high value to ghee. Ghee is hidden in milk, like the potential in creation and of man. By the introduction of "heat" (Agni) to milk, through the friction of churning, butter appears. This butter is then placed over fire and the most hidden part of milk, ghee, is revealed. I think of Agni as the Flame of Aspiration and ghee the symbol of offering up our best intentions and actions. We pour excellence into the Fire and sacrifice our impurities in pursuit of the shining one. The essence of sacrifice is at the heart of all creative forces.

Translations with slight adaptation to RV 6.16.11
Jamison and Brererton 2014

Indian Clarified Butter - Ghee

Ghee is available at Indian and natural groceries and some supermarkets, but you'll learn a new skill and save money by making your own. Ghee is delicious in its purest form, but the infused variations offered here can add a big flavor kick to simple steamed or grilled foods.

Makes about 1 ¾ cups
1 pound (4 sticks) unsalted butter

1. Melt the butter in a heavy-bottomed saucepan over medium heat. Continue to cook until the butter comes to a gentle boil and is covered with foam. Reduce the heat to very low, and gently simmer the butter, uncovered, until the solids have settled to the bottom of the pan and turned from creamy white to rich golden brown, about 45 to 60 minutes. The clear, golden butterfat should be covered with a thin transparent crust. Toward the end of cooking, watch closely to prevent burning.

2. Using a mesh skimmer or slotted spoon remove the crust and set it aside (it may be used in rice dishes or bread dough- store in the refrigerator for up to 3 days) With a ladle, remove all but the bottom ½-inch of clear ghee and pour it through a fine sieve lined with two to three layers of cheesecloth (a paper towel may be used in a pinch) into a clean lidded jar or container. Then pour the rest of the ghee from the pot, stopping just short of the brown solids. The browned solids, if not too dark, may be added to the crusted solids removed from the top or discarded.

3. Let the ghee cool to room temperature then seal the container with a lid. The ghee will keep for a few months at cool to moderate room temperature. When the weather is warm, keep the ghee in the refrigerator.

Flavor-Infused Variations

Ginger Ghee- add a 2-inch piece of fresh ginger, sliced, to the pot along with the butter.

Chile-Cumin Ghee- add 1 to 2 whole dried chiles, such as chile de arbol, chipotle, ancho, or New Mexico and 2 tablespoons whole cumin seeds to the pot along with the butter.

Black Pepper Ghee- add 1 1/2 tablespoons whole black peppercorns to the pot along with the butter.

BREWING SUMERIAN BEER
MARK KELLEY

At the beginning of 2022, the Order of Fire was reading *The Epic of Gilgamesh*, so I started looking around for other interesting findings from the Sumerians, and I found a beer recipe that was translated from Cuneiform, "Hymn to Ninkasi". The hymn leaves out a lot of specifics, but I found that several people have already tried making the beer, so I picked a recipe from someone on the internet and tried it out. My first try was decent, it was malty and refreshing, but the recipe was not very authentic. I wanted to try it again and make it closer to what it might have been like for the Sumerians.

My second try, which is now my own recipe, is what you will see here. I read a book on how to make beer and then I went down the rabbit hole on what we know about the Sumerian method. I made this recipe specifically for an Order of Fire event and will continue to refine it over time.

The recipe and brewing process:

I started with sprouting wheat berries and malted them in the oven, then I ground these by hand into coarse wheat flour.

Next, I made the *bappir*. We do not really know what exactly *bappir* is aside from being baked bread that would have been made with barley. The purpose of the *bappir* was as a bittering agent, which is one purpose of hops in modern beer.

The *bappir* recipe I developed was based on some of the ingredients the Sumerians had available at the time. Being a little short on time I bought malted barley then mixed it with the wheat flour, date syrup, and water. Then I added cardamom, aniseed, and cumin and baked until it was burnt on top.

To get yeast for the brew I went with a more authentic method, I added dates to water and let it sit covered and in the shade for a few days, until it was fermenting nicely.

Now for the actual brewing. The hymn references a mash so this is where I tried to figure out if I should do a hot mash or not. As of today, we have no evidence that Sumerians heated the water for the mash, but they did live in a warm climate, so it was likely that the water was also warm.

I heated my water until it was 105 degrees Fahrenheit and then mixed it all together and stirred it on and off for about 20 minutes, for a little extra sugar I added in the last of the date syrup that I made. The Sumerians brewed their beer in clay pots that were partially buried to keep the water temperature down, so I moved my jar to a shaded part of my kitchen and covered it with cheese cloth.

The result was drunk around the sacred ritual fire during the Holy Round. The beer was very sour but still had a malty aftertaste. The alcohol content did seem to be low, but that was common for the time.

All said and done, I liked this recipe a lot better than the one I followed the first time. I'm sure I will go farther down this rabbit hole before the next Order of Fire event and the recipe will evolve over time.

"'Eat the food, Enkidu, it is the way one lives. Drink the beer, as is the custom of the land.' Enkidu ate the food until he was sated, he drank the beer-seven jugs! and became expansive and sang with joy!"

-Epic of Gilgamesh

Stay Solar.

THE MEANING OF THINGS
THE ROLE OF OBJECTS IN CREATING A MEANINGFUL LIFE
JACK DONOVAN

People surround themselves with disposable, mass-produced items and then complain that their lives lack a sense of meaning...

I'd never argue that objects are more meaningful than people, animals, memories, or even ideas. We'd all agree that if our houses were burning down, we would prioritize saving the people and animals inside – not "things." However, it is not necessary to say that "things never matter" simply to say that people – at least the people we like – matter more.

People, ideas, animals, and objects all contribute to an immersive, multidimensional matrix of meaning and value.

If objects really don't matter at all, why go to a museum?

If buildings and spaces don't matter, why visit historical sites?

There's plenty of marble and gold in the world, but the thing that differentiates THAT gold and THAT marble from all of the other marble and gold on planet Earth is the power of narrative.

Objects and spaces that tell stories enrich our lives.

Imagine inhabiting a space where everything has some kind of narrative.

Years ago, I visited a small Bavarian resort town named Garmisch-Partenkirchen, which has a deeply Catholic history. The buildings are covered with Lüftlmalerei, colorful murals depicting local and religious themes, and there were little nooks in the walls everywhere displaying sculptures of saints and scenes from the Bible. Throughout the town and even along the hiking trails, there are free-standing displays of religious sculptures or painted vignettes of local stories – such as memorials for dead hikers – all framed by high-pitched alpine roofs to remain visible in the winter snow. I was impressed by how immersed the locals were in their history and mythology. One can barely turn one's head there without catching sight of a story.

Garmisch-Partenkirchen is a tourist destination today, and I have no idea how many of the modern Germans who live there are still practicing Catholics. Still, conceptually, it struck me as a spiritual total environment at the scale of a small city. Someone living there during more religious times would feel a sense of total immersion in that belief system.

Having visited Athens recently, I imagine the ancient Athenians might have had a similar sense of being immersed in myth and meaning. There were temples to different gods everywhere, and they were close to markets, public meeting places, and even the state prison.

While creating a sacred city is a big-budget enterprise, we have the ability to create richer lives and sacred spaces by surrounding ourselves with meaningful things.

For this essay, I'm going to create three classifications of meaningful objects:

Aesthetically Meaningful Objects
Symbolically or Representationally Meaningful Objects
Objects with Inherited Narrative
Objects Loaded with Narrative

We could perhaps invent different or additional classifications for meaningful objects, but these should get you started.

Aesthetically Meaningful Objects

True originals – really interesting men – are characters, and characters have style. You could draw them quickly into a graphic novel. They have a vibe that is so distinct that you can easily imagine what kind of vehicle they'd drive, what they'd wear, what their office or gym or "secret lair" looked like. His aesthetic may be elaborate, rugged, or clean and simple, depending on the man's personality and purpose.

Men, especially conservative and masculine men in America, are often discouraged from concerning themselves with aesthetics because visual communication is stigmatized as superficial, non-functional, and effeminate. This is a false dichotomy, much like the idea that people and ideas are meaningful and objects are not, simply because one will naturally take precedence. Function is more important than style and design, but that doesn't mean that design will not enhance or enrich life.

Much of the disdain for design seems puritanical and plebian. I've also written about a psychological dynamic known to anthropologists as "sex pollution." I believe that when women were permitted to become artists and male homosexuality moved from an open secret to a public identity, many lower and middle-class men walled off the art and design worlds as domains for women, communists, and effeminate homosexuals. The result of this, unfortunately, was a world visually designed by and for women, communists, and effeminate homosexuals – not for masculine men.

Men designed everything for most of human history, from functional stone tools to filigree dueling pistols. While examining the overlap between what is beautiful and what is meaningful is beyond the scope of this essay, it seems truthful to say that beauty makes life richer and more meaningful. A sword is a sword, but a beautiful sword is something special. You can build an engine that goes fast, but a Ferarri is more than that.

Developing refined and distinctive tastes distinguishes you as an individual – as a character.

What is your character's aesthetic? The more you experiment visually and inhabit that aesthetic, the more you become that character for yourself and others. Developing a sense of personal style and surrounding yourself with objects that complement that style will help you to "become what you are."

If you've never put a lot of thought into style or design, begin by paying attention to things that "look good" to you and try to figure out why or what you associate with them. Determine how others would describe the visual qualities you find yourself drawn to. Over time, you'll see categories of styles and connections between them and develop a visual literacy that allows you to describe the styles of things that suit your character precisely. Through exploring options, you may also find aesthetic styles and details of things that you've never encountered.

It's like tasting whiskey. You can start with Jack Daniels, but if you try a hundred whiskeys, you'll develop some specific preferences.

Symbolically or Representationally Meaningful Objects

I like the phrase "matrix of meaning" because there is, perhaps with some help of a visual reference to the film series The Matrix, some visual three-dimensionality about it.

We tend to think of meaning as existing solely in our heads – and I suppose that, strictly speaking, it does. However, we are all influenced by objects, sounds, and ideas in our environments. Architects are acutely aware of how different structures make us feel – not just when we look at images of buildings but when we physically walk through them. Different landscapes, colors, and plants all influence our moods and thoughts in different ways.

Earlier in this essay, I described Garmisch-Partenkirchen as a place where a Catholic man would find himself immersed in the mythology that informs him, inspires him, and shapes his identity.

Why not create the same kind of environment for yourself by selecting and collecting objects and artwork that inform, inspire, and shape your identity? If you bring depictions of the myths and ideas that are most meaningful to you into your everyday environment, they will influence you both directly and unconsciously. What is on the walls of the rooms where you spend the most time? What's on your desk or bookshelf? Why isn't it something that depicts or symbolizes your connection to myths or powerful ideas? It doesn't have to be expensive – you can buy framed prints of paintings of almost anything online for under a hundred dollars.

Also, try thinking outside the box to find new ways to immerse yourself in images or ideas that capture your imagination. For an entire year, I hosted grappling matches at my office, during which I projected video of eagles flying over the Alps above us as we rolled. So many men live drab lives surrounded by "default decor" or allow their wives to control the look and feel of the world around them. But contemporary technology enables us to do far more than just put a picture on the wall or a figurine on a desk.

In *The Matrix*, technology created a believable but fictional narrative world as a hamster wheel for the human mind.

In a similar but more positive way, we can use technology to create a narrative world around us – a matrix of meaning – that harmonizes and enhances the conscious and unconscious narratives inside our minds.

Objects with Inherited Narrative

Some objects come with a pre-installed narrative. When people complain that they lack a sense of meaning in life, I suspect that often they feel rootless and lack a sense of connectedness to a culture and heritage that they might have in a more traditional or tribal society. Using objects your mother, father, and grandparents used creates a sense of continuity and groundedness that you can't get from something you bought at the store. Objects that tell the story of your family's history, especially if you have relatives who have done curious or impressive things, make your own story more interesting and establish your place in an ongoing saga.

That said, not everyone inherits significant objects or stories, and many may want to distinguish themselves from an unremarkable history or separate themselves from the deeds or ideas of forefathers who "missed the mark."

We can surround ourselves with objects that have been part of the stories of the kinds of men we admire. Of course, the items showcased in museums and historical sites often have the best or most familiar stories. Still, one can affordably acquire all sorts of objects that come with their own implied or documented stories online or at antique stores. Signed books, objects that belonged to someone important, objects that have been involved in military campaigns or operations, objects of art from visionary artists, and even objects from archeological finds. There are so many Roman coins in the world that they can be purchased cheaply. If you want to invoke the spirit of a particular region, you can easily import something from that area. Even prehistoric objects are accessible. One of my old ritual garments has a 25,000-year-old fossilized tooth of a cave bear attached to it. You can acquire such a thing for under a hundred dollars.

Some objects inherit a story "accidentally." The first example that comes to mind is an athlete who becomes superstitious about a pair of lucky socks or underwear or a piece of uniform or equipment that has become part of his winning streak. An object can acquire the resonance of a positive or negative memory if it was present during a meaningful event.

A souvenir might fall into this category – whether it was an item purchased in a gift shop or perhaps just a stone or a pinecone you picked up during a memorable hike or adventure. "Souvenir" is a French verb meaning "to remember." The noun form indicates an object that helps you to remember something. Surrounding yourself or even carrying objects with you that trigger memories will naturally help everyday life feel richer and more meaningful.

Sacred Things – Objects Loaded with Narrative

Finally, we are not limited to acquiring objects with existing visual or historical narratives or waiting for something to acquire a story accidentally. We can intentionally "load" objects with narrative.

Giving a thing a name means giving it a story and making a rule that defines it and separates it from other things.

Calling a hunk of sandstone a "rock" differentiates it from trees, dirt, and other parts of the landscape.

The distinctive characteristics of a particular rock give it character and add to the story of the rock. How heavy is the rock? Is its surface jagged or smooth? How old is the rock? Was it once a piece of that mountain over there? If I lift the rock, it becomes the rock that I lifted. If I kill something with the rock, the rock is both a rock and a weapon.

To make an object special or sacred, you develop its character and narrative. A wedding ring is a simple example of a sacred object that has been intentionally loaded with narrative.

To make a wedding ring, you select the ring and indicate that it is a wedding ring – and not some decorative ring or fashion accessory. You separate the wedding ring from all other rings and magically pronounce that ring to be a wedding ring – a physical symbol of what is still generally assumed to be a lifelong bond of marriage between a man and a woman.

By naming it or calling it a wedding ring, you load it with a broader cultural understanding of what marriage is and connect it somehow to all other wedding rings and the intangible Platonic form of a wedding ring. This ring – which was once part of a rock and which you probably purchased in a store – is now very important, and you keep it safe until the date of the wedding. If you were to forget to bring the ring to the wedding, it would throw off the whole ritual.

Assuming that you remembered to bring it to the wedding – the magical wedding ritual is performed, and the couple is pronounced "husband and wife." The man and the woman get new, special titles during this magical ritual, their families are officially united, and the woman usually takes the last name of the husband's paternal line. Both the husband and wife achieve a change in social status and move into a different phase of life with particular roles and obligations.

The bond is sealed, and the ring is placed on someone's finger. While wedding rings are sometimes removed, the man and woman are expected to wear them daily and display them so that others recognize that they are married. The wedding ring now carries not only the meaning of marriage but the story of the wedding ritual and the day of the wedding, and it accumulates the history of the marriage. If the marriage ends, the wedding rings are removed. Perhaps they are sold and melted back into precious metal that will be used to make something else.

One can make any object or space sacred by following essentially the same formula:

Set it Apart - Set the object or space apart and indicate that it is sacred.

Give It a Sacred Name - You may or may not give it a special name. Regardless, it will likely undergo a state change requiring a definite article rather than an indefinite one. What is "a" cup will become "the" cup.

Connect it to a Form - The object becomes a symbol of an abstract form and acquires its history and cultural associations. If the cup becomes a ritual cup, it is then connected to particular and general stories about ritual cups. It becomes part of the narrative of ritual cups. And, assuming it is being used for a specific ritual in a particular group, it acquires a place in the context of those ritual cups and those rituals and that group.

Customize it (Optional) - If the object was made custom or crafted with intent, this adds another layer of narrative – perhaps even visual and structural narrative, if it is covered with images or symbols.

Give It a Story and a History of Its Own - The object may or may not be used, like a wedding ring, for a particular ritual. Perhaps it is merely an object for meditation and reflection. If you were to use the same object for meditation and reflection every day for a year, it would absorb a certain resonance and carry the history of that. The sacred object would become more important than it was on the first day.

You can develop an object's story by taking it to meaningful places or making it part of important events. Take it to the top of a mountain or carry it on an adventure. Bring it to an ancient site. Have it present during a major life change. Have the sacred object signed or marked or blessed in some way by someone relevant to its purpose. Imagine that you were writing the description of your sacred object for an explanatory plaque in a museum or a descriptive passage in a book. What would you want it to say? If you can, turn that fantasy into a reality.

Protect Its Narrative - You may want to protect your sacred object from mundane events or scenarios that you perceive to be profane or obscene in some way. Keep it stored in a special box or a safe and bring it out and use it only for very specific occasions. This may feel more necessary for some objects than others. Follow your gut on this unless there's a particular convention you admire.

* * *

Intentionally building a more meaningful life requires creative thought and commitment. If you want the story of your life to be interesting – not only to others but to yourself – start thinking and acting as your own creator. Stop receiving all of your stories and start writing more of them. Become a novelist writing the story of your life.

What kinds of things are part of your character's world, and what kinds of stories do those things have?

SOLSTICE
CHRISTOPHER HEALEY

One of the oldest Christmas traditions I know is lecturing other people about the true meaning of Christmas. Of the many festivals & celebrations observed in Europe throughout the year, it's the one which, in its place in the drama of the seasons is self-evidently solemn & significant.

Despite living in an age where we have effectively vanquished the darkness indefinitely & live through the winter in an eternal midsummer in our homes I think our biology hasn't quite moved on yet, which explains the almost universal response we have to the darkest day & the subtle rebirth that follows.

Men through the ages have tried to rationalise this response, wrapped it in religion & culture. A kaleidoscope of images. But ultimately, for me, it's a return to a primordial starting point.

The fire in the dark.

The gloom of winter is fertile soil for man's defining quality, his imagination to bloom. Fearful men imagine monsters & spectres on the periphery of their perception. Others understand & trust that the light will return & the darkness is a canvas for their bold plans

& fantasies about the year ahead. The biting cold & icy weather, the mounds of accumulating snow, the damp & floods galvanises them, hardens them, ready to put those plans into action inch by inch with the same gradual, yet incessant way that the sun returns to increasing illuminate the spoils of our efforts.

As a period of renewal, we show gratitude to each other & share the abundance of the previous cycle with the confidence that we are already on the path to create more.

The physiological impetus towards the winter solstice is, perhaps our most tangible cultural tie to prehistory as well as our future. The small things we do in the dark, mount up to the glorious things we enjoy at midsummer.

THE MEANING OF A SOLAR YEAR
VIC VERDIER

What's more usual and normal than the calendar we use every day? Every past and present civilization looked for a way to record or celebrate specific events, based on religion, agriculture, politics or Nature.

Since the Egyptians, most calendars have a year trying to approximate the movement of the Sun. Other calendars are based on the Moon, like the one most often used in the Islam world. Finally a few calendars are lunisolars, mixing the solar concept with some lunar adaptations.

Apparently no civilization ever used a Pluto-based calendar because it has a 495 year orbit around the Sun and that would make the concept of life-year pretty useless. A Mercury-based calendar (88 day cycle) would make me a 245 year-old man and I would rather have my age in dog years. So even if a Solar calendar is just a convention, it's a convention based on a star we have been praying to for the dawn of age.

The calendar we are the most familiar with is the Gregorian calendar, introduced by pope Gregory XIII in the 16th century, based on the Julian calendar - named after Julius Caesar, the egotistic Roman

Emperor - with some obvious Catholic twists.

What's wrong with it? A lot actually.

First of all, its epoch - the year it starts - is when Jesus of Nazareth was born, a date that has no significance whatsoever for non-Christian countries but was adopted nonetheless almost worldwide, just to facilitate international travels and transactions. It seems trivial as 2023 is what we are sued to, but we are in year 5783 in the Jewish world, year 4 in Reiwa era Japan, year 1444 AH in the Muslim world, and the Chinese are ready to celebrate New Year, a date that changes every year since it started almost 3000 years ago.

As we speak about New Year, there is nothing really solar in the Gregorian January 1st. As a matter of fact, in pretty much the whole world, the beginning of the year has always been at different dates. Solar events - like solstice or equinox - were often used as a starting day. And because the Julian calendar was used as a base for the Gregorian one, even the name of the months we constantly use, are the living remains of those times. The first months are based on Roman divinities or Emperors (Janus, Februa, Mars, Aphrodite, Maia, Juno, Julius Cesar and Augustus), but the last months show a clear difference between their names and their places in the Gregorian calendar (Seventh, Eighth, Nineth and Tenth months).

The christian origin of the seven-day week is more questionable, and even if the Bible clearly defines it at the beginning of the Genesis - setting up the 7th day as the rest day - it seems that the Persians, the Greeks and the Chinese used the same idea well before the Hebrews. Other past religions seemed to have more hard-working Gods who only needed a rest day every 8 or 10 days.

So what would be a good Solar calendar that is not deeply tainted by the old religions? I'm maybe not very objective - or serious - but I would say that the French Revolution had a pretty good one, rejecting every single religious concept or celebration, making it extremely simple and copying what Nature and the planets would determine: You had 12 months a year, each of them being 30 days long, and 3 weeks of 10 days per month. You add to that between 5 and 6 days at the end of the year to take into account the variations of the Sun from one year to the next. And of course, in a typical French tradition, these few extra days were used for extreme libations and parties. Think "The Purge" with a lot of wine and cheese.

This calendar started on the day of the autumnal equinox, and the names of the 12 months were poetically chosen to highlight the relationship between Men and Nature, the weather, and the major agricultural tasks to be done: vintage, mist, frost, snow, rain, wind, flower, meadow, harvest, heat, etc. Sounds pretty Solar to me!

Unfortunately the Revolutionary Calendar was only used for 12 years, as it was abolished as soon as a Corsican general decided to become Emperor. Like most things in France, good ideas are never taken seriously. Like this article.

THE SPIRITUAL ORIGINS OF SCIENCE
C.B. ROBERTSON

"Spirit" is not a word commonly paired with science. To the lay public, science is presented as a near-opposite to all things "spiritual"—rational, analytical, empirical, and above all, skeptical. To consult science is to set aside myth, to banish superstition and prejudice in favor of clear thinking and reason, in hopes of landing upon a more accurate vision of reality.

In its historical and original form, science was first an individual, spiritual undertaking.

Today, institutions lay claim to every achievement once created in the spirit of science, and from this claim assert the right to speak for science itself. They advance a "social technology" model of science, arguing that peer-review and expert consensus are the essential core to "real" science. This places professional experts in a place of epistemological power, like priests in a hierarchical religious institution. And as with priests, cultural and political power comes along with this claimed privileged access to truth.

But if science has an underlying spirit, then the institutional claims to the honorable mantle of "science" is both false and more deeply "anti-science" than any of the supposedly anti-scientific theories we see today.

It is the purpose of this essay to explain this spiritual dimension of science.

To begin this exploration, we might ask: why should a man engage in science in the first place? Why pursue a more objective vision of reality?

A common answer is that science provides us with material benefits and a higher standard of living.

Biologist Richard Dawkins famously argued that "it works; planes fly, cars drive, computers compute. If you base medicine on science, you cure people. If you base the design of planes on science, they fly."

But much of our modern world works just fine without science. We do not need to understand the true nature of things, or have falsifiable working models in order to invent and create by trial and error. Romans built roads and aqueducts and bridges unparalleled for a thousand years without Bacon's scientific method. Electrical engineers today cannot even agree on which direction electricity moves in a circuit, yet this does not prevent us from lighting the civilized world with its power. Endlessly pursuing a more objective view of the world is almost always superfluous.

The vast majority of science brings us no real economic benefit to offset its research cost. Studying the mating habits of a particular endangered tortoise, or the properties of light near dense gravity, do not make planes fly or computers compute. Most science is not done for — or justified by — its effects on our standard of living. By this measure, the vast majority of science would be considered a waste of time and money.

Rather, the true justification for science is the pursuit of knowledge for its own sake.

My favorite example of this is Justin O. Schmidt, an entomologist who studied honey bees. Frustrated by the absence of any systematic comparison of different insect stings, Schmidt decided to establish a baseline himself. Schmidt spent years getting stung by all variety of insects, in all variety of unpleasant parts of his own body, rating the pain on a scale of 1-4.

One might wonder what value could come from such a scale, but to distinguish between "useful" knowledge and "useless" knowledge is itself a subjective assertion. Seeking to understand the world through systematic empiricism—through science—is in some sense to disregard the distinction between "useful" and "useles," where knowledge is concerned—to see facts as facts, neither good nor bad; useful nor useless.

In addition to ratings, Schmidt added descriptions of the quality of the stings. In the pain level 4 category was the warrior wasp, which Schmidt described in the following language: "Torture. You are chained in the flow of an active volcano. Why did I start this list?"

Of course, Schmidt could have asked this question at the start, before stinging himself with the most painful insects known to man. Why pursue an objective view of reality, when a subjective view is perfectly functional (stereotypes and prejudices are sometimes useful), when much objective knowledge is useless and when a truly objective view is impossible anyhow?

The modern advocates of science aren't very good at answering such a question – especially in the face of material discomfort that perfectly opposes the high standard of living and comfort so often used to justify science.

But to ask the question "why do science?" in the context of stinging oneself with various insects is to simultaneously ask the related question: "what is science?" Is what Schmidt was doing "real" science, and if not, what does the real thing look like?

Most people understand science to be synonymous with the "scientific method," a systematic process of exploring the world through observation, prediction, testing, and analysis. But aside from the most general of descriptions, this "method" is not singular. Paul Feyerabend, the Swiss philosopher of science, even argued that strict methodology was opposed to science and scientific progress:

> The idea of a method that contains firm, unchanging, and absolutely binding principles for conducting the business of science meets considerable difficulty when confronted with the results of historical research. We find, then, that there is not a single rule, however plausible, and however firmly grounded in epistemology, that is not violated at some time or other. It becomes evident that such violations are not accidental events, they are not results of insufficient knowledge or of inattention which might have been avoided. On the contrary, we see that they are necessary for progress. (*Against Method*, 1975)

Descriptively, there is no singular "scientific method" that one can use to distinguish science from pseudoscience or non-science.

Some fields of science do not permit experimentation – paleontology, for instance. One can only make predictions based on hypotheses, and see what shows up. Some might say that such fields cannot even be properly called "science," but such a charge opens the doorway to the purity-spiral of relative "hardness," which quickly excludes psychology, anthropology, and economics from the domain of "real science."

And even among the "hard sciences," method is not universal. One does not test a mathematical formula in the same way one explores a chemical compound. Standards for exactitude and rigor vary depending upon what the field permits.

This is how someone describing the sting of a bald-faced hornet as "rich, hearty, slightly crunchy [...] similar to getting your hand mashed in a revolving door" can be scientific. Subjective descriptions like that of a wine-connoisseur are not rigorous in the manner of a geometric equation, but they establish a baseline which others can build on top of with increasing precision over time (we are still waiting for replication of Schmidt's pain experiences), just as the primitive exploration of numbers thousands of years ago paved the way for more precise and complex mathematics today.

What defines this method as science is not the precise steps or procedure, but rather a kind of inquisitive spirit which informs its construction in context. This spirit of science is not merely the cause of maximizing exactitude and objectivity in whatever inquiry the scientist engages, but also the *why* behind the exploration in the first place.

This spirit of science has a history we can explore.

Friedrich Nietzsche argued that Socrates was the originator of what was eventually to become the scientific spirit. In *The Birth of Tragedy*, Nietzsche said:

> [...] Socrates is the archetype of the theoretical optimist, who in the above-indicated belief in the fathomableness of the nature of things, attributes to knowledge and perception the power of a universal medicine, and sees in error and evil. To penetrate into the depths of the nature of things, and to separate true perception from error and illusion, appeared to the Socratic man the noblest and even the only truly human calling: just as from the time of Socrates onwards the mechanism of concepts, judgments, and inferences was prized above all other capacities as the highest activity and the most admirable gift of nature. (1871)

Socrates was in many ways the prototype of the scientific culture, endlessly criticizing those who claimed knowledge, though rarely advancing opinions of his own. A walking, one-man peer-review machine, he endlessly challenged others in the hopes that what could survive such scrutiny would be more reliable knowledge.

But here, to focus on Socrates' strategy and the utility of his means for inquiry would be to miss the true spirit itself, and the aesthetic belief which gives it life:

To pursue knowledge is good for its own sake.

Many centuries later, Gotthold Ephraim Lessing poetically described this sentiment in the following manner:

> The true value of a man is not determined by his possession, supposed or real, of Truth, but rather by his sincere exertion to get to the Truth. It is not possession of the Truth, but rather the pursuit of Truth by which he extends his powers and in which his ever-growing perfectibility is to be found. Possession makes one passive, indolent, and proud. If God were to hold all Truth concealed in his right hand, and in his left only the steady and diligent drive for Truth, albeit with the proviso that I would always and forever err in the process, and offer me the choice, I would with all humility take the left hand, and say: Father, I will take this one—the pure Truth is for You alone. (1778)

Lessing's depiction is of the pursuit of knowledge as a means to the end of moral virtue... or perhaps as an indicator and expression of virtue. But in either case it depicts the pursuit of knowledge—and not the acquisition of purported facts—as the aim and value of science. It is this curiosity and hunger for knowledge that the activity of science, in all of its variety of method, seeks to satiate.

The true spirit of science is a hunger to know, not to be satisfied with knowledge that is merely functional, but to truly understand for the sake of understanding.

Christian monks of the medieval ages pursued science as an outgrowth of natural theology: the idea being that though God remains separated and hidden from man, man can seek his Creator and come to know Him by exploring creation.

Here, the undertaking of science was explicitly religious, not as a means of developing virtue but as the right and natural relationship between a created being and his Creator. One could say the same thing in a less denominational fashion—that it is right for a human being gifted with intellect and curiosity to explore and pursue what is objective and transcendent, not because it is useful, but because we can – just as it would be a shame to never exercise and develop the muscles our bodies have been blessed with.

> Repugnant is the creature who would squander the ability
>
> To lift an eye to heaven, conscious of his fleeting time here
>
> (TOOL)

This hunger for knowledge is the spirit of science. It is the pursuit of knowledge for its own sake that drives increasingly precise and thorough standards that have come to characterize scientific methods. This spirit is an individual matter, as it relates to an individual's relationship with the universe, with God, with the transcendent, or else a matter of developing the individual's virtue in humility, diligence, care, and even gratitude and reverence.

It may be true that it is harder to be in awe before a thing rendered transparent by exploration, but very little reveals the true mystery that surrounds us as quickly as testing what we think we know.

Here, the Greek language helps encapsulate this spirit in the history of important scientific words. The word "theory" derives from the Greek theōriā, which means 'sacred journey.' Harvard philologist Gregory Nagy describes its root theōros in the following way:

> Etymologically, theōros means 'one who sees [root hor-] a vision [theā].' So the basic meaning of theōriā can be reconstructed as a ritualized journey undertaken for the purpose of achieving a sacralized vision. (*The Ancient Greek Hero in 24 Hours*, 2013)

A great deal has changed in the way we use "theory" today. But for all that change, a "theory" is still a kind of vision of reality, and sacred in the sense that it is held as special, above ordinary opinion because of the journey – the ritualized scientific process of experimentation, analysis, etc – by which that vision was assembled. One could also say that a "theory" itself is a journey, a model-in-motion that adapts to new information.

But in the spirit of science, the most important journey is not the one made to acquire a particular vision (the method), or the journey of the vision (the theory), but that of the individual scientist in his efforts to see more clearly.

Yet in the days of Socrates, such an individual hunger for knowledge could be politically subversive. In Plato's *Apology*, Socrates has to ask the crowd not to interrupt with indignant outbursts as he recounts his friend Chaerephon's unsanctioned journey to the Oracle of Delphi—in those days, only a "sacred delegate" of the city (the more literal meaning of *theōros*) was supposed to consult the oracle. Even Socrates called his friend's journey "bold" and his friend "very impetuous in all his doings."

Historically, these bold and impetuous individuals are the source of almost all scientific innovation and progress. Great advancements like those of Galileo, Newton, Darwin, Tesla, or the Wright brothers were the result of obsessive individuals exploring in relative isolation, often under the disapproving eyes of the institutions of their day.

In today's day and age, the spirit of science retains its political subversiveness. Galileo is sometimes mentioned as a conveniently distant example of the persecutions suffered by scientists who did not show due deference to political power (perhaps in hopes of insinuating that such persecutions are a matter of the distant past). But examples of censorship, blacklisting, and more serious forms of persecution of those charged with corrupting the minds of the youth carry on to this day, often under the guise of *science*.

As recently as December of 2021, *Scientific American* published an article defaming the still-warm body of E.O. Wilson as a racist with problematic ideas. The author argued that to engage with "scientistis whose legacy is complicated," certain steps should be taken so that people don't get the wrong political idea from scientific work which does not account for political interests. "[T]ruth and reconciliation are necessary in the scientific record, including attention to citational practices when using or reporting on problematic work. This approach includes thinking critically about where and when to include historically problematic work..." In laymen's terms, Scientific American is recommending a culture of censorship, of deleting the work of "problematic" scientists from journals, periodicals, and even textbooks—or if a "problematic" person must be included in the record, that they be presented with "the context necessary for readers to understand the limitations of the ideas embedded in it." Presumably, this necessary context would include an exhortation to dismiss in advance the opinions of the scientist in question.

That this classical form of political censorship and moral condemnation could take place under the guise of "science" is a symptom of a more modern innovation: the "social technology" model of science.

In his book *Kindly Inquisitors*, Jonathan Rauch described science as a social model, appending "liberal" before the term "science" to denote it as a social institution for dispute-resolution and generating political legitimacy in matters of knowledge, rather than merely seeking facts for their own sake. "Liberal science [...] is a way of organizing society and a way of behaving" (1993).

"Liberal science" – science as a social technology – takes the view that science produces a reliable path to knowledge because external criticism and peer review serves as a better check against bad ideas than reviewing our own ideas.

There is certainly some wisdom in this.

But scientific legitimacy is only one standard of truth or value. Human history is replete with values such as beauty, honor, and liberty, which have no basis in science. Cognitive psychologist Steven Pinker once said that honor is 'that curious thing which we believe exists because we believe everyone else believes it exists.'

The nature of subjective or localized values is such that they are often invisible to scientific inquiry. What is universal is not always "more true" than what is particular, but it is often a lower common denominator in quality. Speaking of television, David Foster Wallace said that the breadth of the audience necessarily tended toward lower and lower quality of entertainment:

> TV is the epitome of low art in its desire to appeal to and enjoy the attention of unprecedented numbers of people. But TV is not low because it is vulgar or prurient or stupid. It is often all these things, but this is a logical function of its need to please Audience. And I'm not saying that television is vulgar and dumb because the people who compose Audience are vulgar and dumb. Television is the way it is simply because people tend to be really similar in their vulgar and prurient and stupid interests and wildly different in their refined and moral and intelligent interests (E Unibas Pluram, 1993)

When performed by an individual, pursuing science for individual reasons (perhaps as an expression of an irrepressible need to know things), it is easy for that individual to relegate scientific facts and epistemology to its appropriate place in his own value-hierarchy. He can value the facts, while still subjugating his knowledge of the facts to his feelings of love, loyalty, or duty.

When scientific institutions come together—as they inevitably must, when the demand for peer evaluation becomes high enough—scientific epistemology must be the sole unifying force. Non-scientific values are relegated to the periphery or discounted as "unscientific," and the power of consensus leaves little room for individual judgment over which values are most important.

Even these scientific institutions are willing to condescend and mouth platitudes about the importance of art and literature and other matters... at least in times of peace. But when hard choices have to be made – for instance, between something as unmeasurable and subjective as "freedom" and something as concrete as health or temperature – the pressure of scientific institutions will always be towards the lowest common denominator. Liberal science will always choose the measurable, even if the hearts of individual scientists hold reservations.

We might, for instance, hear something saccharine and conciliatory about the "independent spirit" of America, before being told that "now is the time to do as you're told."

This tendency becomes fractally pernicious when it is applied to the evaluating the "reasonableness" of citizens. The motivations which science cannot see—by nature of its materialistic limitations in vision—will make perfectly normal people appear irrational to scientific institutions. Anyone who cares about honor, for instance, may be dismissed as a backwards barbarian, trapped in an ancient mind-game of violence, and whose opinion can have no bearing on the function of a civilized society. It isn't long before this perceived irrationality grows into an outright contempt for the lay public, who must be manipulated with "noble lies" because they cannot possibly understand the science. The institution's inherent blindness to non-scientific (but not un-scientific) values leads to an utter inability to comprehend the nature of outsider's skepticism. The institutions inevitably pathologize the entire world as irrational or stupid, mistaking their own incomprehension from their own epistemologically-limited scope for the intellectual limitations of others.

For example, in March of 2020, *PLOS Biology* defined "an antiscience movement" as "...an organized and funded rejection of science and scientific principles and methods in factor of alternative views, often linked to the targeting or harassment of individual scientists." A year later, *Scientific American* claimed that "antiscience is the rejection of mainstream scientific views and methods or their replacement with unproven or deliberately misleading theories, often for nefarious and political gains."

This is, of course, neither the nature of science-skepticism, nor why people are increasingly skeptical of scientific experts.

People distrust science—as curated by the institutions and the media—because of a natural, healthy, human distrust of conflicting interests and the transparency and purity of anything remotely political. But such reasoning is not made in the appropriately scientific language, and is argued from outside the scientific epistemological framework. Thus, it is not acknowledged by scientific institutions, and the skeptic can only be seen as unreasonable, nefarious, or both.

This brings us full-circle to the spirit of science.

Much of the philosophy of science in the 20th century was framed in opposition to Plato's *Republic*. Karl Popper wrote *The Open Society* largely in opposition to the totalitarian censorship-state depicted by Plato as the "just city." Jonathan Rauch describes reading the *Republic* as coming "face to face with the ethic of a totalitarian regime."

But Plato's *Republic* does not advocate totalitarianism.

In a conversation exploring the nature of justice, Plato's characters construct a theoretical city as an abstract analogue to better understand justice in the context of the individual:

> "I'll tell you," I said. "There is, we say, justice of one man; and there is, surely, justice of a whole city too?"
> "Certainly," he said. [...]
> "So then, perhaps there would be more justice in the bigger and it would be easier to observe closely. If you want, first we'll investigate what justice is like in the cities. Then, we'll also go on to consider it in individuals, considering the likeness of the bigger in the idea of the littler? (*Republic*, Book II)

When Plato describes the just city as being ruled by a philosopher king, he is speaking metaphorically of an individual and that individual's passionate desire for knowledge and wisdom. The limits of this metaphor are later made explicit, when the characters describe the various ways in which such a just city could never actually exist and would inevitably fail as a city.

And if there was any doubt left as to the intended subject-matter of *Republic*, Plato concludes with a cryptic story about reincarnated souls choosing their next lives, and the importance of justice in this process.

The *Republic* is – at the beginning and the end – about the individual choosing the good life at the expense of the political life, just as Plato's teacher Socrates had done:

> ...he who will really fight for the right, if he would live even for a little while, must have a private station and not a public one. (*Apology*)

The consistent misunderstanding of so obvious a message is both a symptom of the scientific institutional mindset, and an example of why much of the lay public would mistrust the supposed expertise of those who advocate for science in politics. Even an advocate of science like Karl Popper believed that Plato was arguing for "the establishment of a state which is free from the evils of all other states because it does not degenerate, because it does not change" (*The Open Society and its Enemies*, 1962).

In reality, Plato was advocating the individual pursuit of wisdom, regardless of – and perhaps, like Socrates, even in opposition to – the state.

In short, Plato was advocating the individual pursuit of the spirit of science.

The misunderstanding of Plato reveals something unscientific in the development of scientific institutions. They limit the capacity of those they influence to perceive certain kinds of knowledge, and they even crush the inquisitive heart of those around them.

In *The Demon-Haunted World*, Carl Sagan described an instance in which he disheartened a taxi-driver who had taken an interest in Atlantis and UFOs, giant kraken and advanced ancient civilizations. Each subject the man brought up, Sagan dismissed as unscientific and fundamentally lacking any substantive evidence. Sagan wrote:

> As far as science can tell, they never existed. By now a little reluctantly, I told him so.

As we drove through the rain, I could see him getting glummer and glummer. I was dismissing not just some errant doctrine, but a precious facet of his inner life. (1997)

We may think it right to dismiss a such a facet of a man's inner life if it concerns fanciful stories dressed up in the guise of archeology.

But what if the man had been speaking not of UFOs, but of honor?

What if, like Socrates, the taxi-driver had been enthusiastically conversing about justice?

About free will?

About a spirit that sought knowledge for its own sake?

Would Carl Sagan have reluctantly informed him that such things did not exist?

We have seen Steven Pinker speak along these lines, and Karl Popper misunderstand Plato so fantastically as to miss the point entirely.

The "real scientist" – the man who truly embodies the spirit of science

– is not driving down political main-street, correcting everyone who he believes to be wrong about something.

He is more likely to be out in the woods somewhere, documenting the flavor of a fire-ant sting, to satisfy his own curiosity (perhaps after doing some reading to see if someone else had already gone through that pain).

By virtue of his individuality and curiosity, he is also more likely to understand Plato's *Republic*, which means that he is more likely to understand himself, others, and what it means to be human.

At the end of the day, the good things we receive from science – as well as the goodness of science itself – are contingent upon this scientific spirit which precedes the method and institutions with which we identify science today. This spirit is one of "impetuous" curiosity and the desire for a personal connection with the objective and the transcendent, unmediated by a priestly caste of institutionally-ordained experts.

We may say that it is "unscientific" or "anti-scientific" to contradict a given theory of science, or to question the holistic validity of the scientific method. But insofar as theories derive from method, and method derives from the scientific spirit, there can be nothing more un-scientific than to contradict or corrode this spirit.

ARCHITECTURE AND SOLAR IDEALISM
VIC VERDIER

As someone who mostly slept in dodgy hotel rooms and bedbug infested AirBnBs all his life, the convenience and functionality of a dwelling, and not its esthetic, has always been a priority for me. That never stopped from always being fascinated by what different civilizations designed and built, and how architecture mostly reflected human ingenuity and innovation, with designs drawing inspiration from various sources in the natural world. Among these inspirations, the Sun has long been a source of fascination and influence for architects around the world, incorporating it into their architecture, not only for practical purposes but also as a symbol of spiritual significance. Its radiant energy, awe-inspiring visual qualities, and vital role in sustaining life have all contributed to its status as a muse for architectural design.

Sun Worship and Ancient Architecture

The Sun holds a special place in the history of human civilization, with many ancient cultures incorporating Sun worship into their belief systems. As a result, these civilizations often designed architectural marvels that paid tribute to the Sun and demonstrate how its path across the sky influenced the design of religious buildings in different parts of the world.

The Egyptian temple of Abu Simbel, built during the reign of Pharaoh Ramses II, is precisely aligned so that, twice a year, the rising Sun illuminates the inner sanctum, casting light on statues of the gods Ra, Amun, and Ramses himself.

The Mayans constructed pyramids and temples, such as El Castillo at Chichen Itza, with architectural features that align with the solstices to celebrate the Sun's movements.

CHICHEN ITZA. ADOBE STOCK

Stonehenge, a Neolithic monument in England, is perhaps one of the most famous examples of solar alignment, as it is arranged so that the rising Sun aligns with the Heel Stone on the summer solstice, creating a breathtaking celestial spectacle. This alignment served both as a spiritual symbol and as a practical calendar for agricultural purposes.

In the heart of the Aztec capital of Tenochtitlan, Templo Mayor was dedicated to the Sun-God Huitzilopochtli. Its orientation and construction included symbolism related to the Sun's daily and annual journey across the sky.

The Inca city of Machu Picchu in Peru features a unique Intihuatana stone, which was believed to capture the Sun's energy and was used for agricultural and spiritual purposes. The design of this stone aligns with the movement of the Sun and the stars, emphasizing the Inca's spiritual connection with the celestial bodies.

Newgrange, in Ireland, is a Neolithic burial mound. It was designed so that, during the winter solstice, a narrow beam of sunlight penetrates the structure's entrance and illuminates the central chamber. This spectacular event highlights the importance of solar symbolism and the cyclical nature of life and death.

NEWGRANGE. ADOBE STOCK

Ancient architecture is a testament to the rich tapestry of human history, culture, and spirituality. The Sun's role in ancient architecture went beyond mere utilitarian considerations; it was a symbol of divinity, timekeeping, and the cyclical nature of life and death. The precise alignments, solar pathways, and celestial phenomena incorporated into these structures are a testament to the advanced astronomical knowledge and spiritual connection that these ancient civilizations had with the Sun.

Solar Idealism in modern architecture

The decline of Sun worship in the ancient Western world started with the Greeks. Their god Helios - and his Roman counterpart Sol - never was a major player in their Pantheon, mostly venerated locally and for major astronomical events like the Panathenaic Games, held in honor of Athena, that often coincided with significant solar events every 4 years.

In both the Greek and the Roman world, the Sun was plentiful and had a much more practical use: warming up buildings and providing light. The idea of passive solar building design first appeared in Greece around the 5th century BC. Up until that time, the Greeks' main source of fuel had been charcoal, but due to a major shortage of wood to burn, they were forced to find a new way of heating their dwellings. The Greeks revolutionized the design of their cities when they began using building materials that absorbed solar energy, mostly stone, and started orienting the buildings so that they faced south.

From now on, western civilizations focused on using the Sun as a practical tool for comfort, somehow forgetting its symbolism. Even in the 15th century, when Copernicus and Galileo championed heliocentrism, the fact that the Earth is not at the center of the Universe, the Sun didn't recover its religious significance, proving again how effective the censorship of the Catholic Church was.

Then the question becomes: what would make a building Solar and is there any example of Solar architecture in the last few hundred years?

To answer this question, let's go back to Jack Donovan's "Manifesto of Solar Culture":

"Solar Culture is inspired by the primal, archetypal past and the myths and aesthetic elements from historical cultures. The challenge of Solar culture is to remix the primal, mythic past and synthesize it into a vision of the future. Solar culture is forward-thinking and future-primitive."

If the Solar Culture prefers light over darkness, it is interesting to note that the Dark Ages were aptly named and represent a time where the role of the Sun became less important in architecture. Most building were self-centered, facing inward to provide more defense against invaders, either domestic or foreign. The ordenburgen, the castles built throughout Europe by the various religious and military Orders, crusaders, and brotherhoods, kept the sunlight out and the germs in.

It's only when the Italian Renaissance spreads over the Old Continent, during the cultural and artistic movement that spanned the 14th to the 17th century, that the Sun made its come-back with large windows lighting up large rooms. Most cathedrals of this period, like the iconic dome of Florence's Cathedral, Santa Maria del Fiore, use natural light, guided by strategically placed windows, to illuminate the frescoes decorating the interior.

It will culminate with architectural wonders like Versailles, the palace built near Paris to celebrate the god-like cult of the Sun-King Louis XIV, despite his questionable high heels and long curly wigs.

VERSAILLES. ADOBE STOCK

But Solar architecture will only find its true meaning a couple of hundred years later, after the Napoleonic wars and the popular revolutions that kept European countries busy and bloody for a while.

At the end of the 19th century, new artistic movements were born, first in Europe, then in the US. In Spain, one of my favorite architects, the Catalan Antoni Gaudi, used the Sun and its light as a constant in his Art Nouveau-influenced buildings, dwellings, and parks, and later in Barcelona's most eccentric cathedral, The Sagrada Familia.

With the technological progress that came after the industrial revolution, men were also able to focus their architectural efforts on taller and more imposing buildings. That's when the first neoclassical skyscrapers were built in Chicago, seemingly reaching the Sun and defying anything else that has been erected before. Then the Art Deco movement, born in France but widely used and improved in New York city, inspired the architects who built most skyscrapers in the 1920s, from the Empire State Building to the Chrysler tower.

Shortly after, architects like Frank Lloyd Wright and Richard Neutra embraced the Sun as a design partner, allowing it to shape the character of private dwellings and integrating them with their natural surroundings.

A couple of decades later, Brutalism, the architectural movement known for its bold use of raw concrete and imposing structures, also found an unexpected ally in the Sun. While the monolithic and often stark nature of brutalist buildings might seem at odds with the warmth of sunlight, the Sun's journey across the sky introduced an ever-changing aspect to brutalist architecture. For instance, the Swiss architect Le Corbusier used the long shadows cast by the buildings, when the winter Sun sits lower in the sky, to create dramatic and elongated forms, that contrast with the harsh overhead light of the summer.

Finally, and more recently, several iconic structures fully embrace the Sun as the main component of their design. The Sydney Opera House, designed by the Danish architect Jorn Utzon, features a series of shell-like structures that capture and reflect sunlight, creating an interplay of light and shadow. Similarly, the Guggenheim Museum in Bilbao, designed by Frank Gehry, uses the reflective properties of its titanium cladding to interact with sunlight throughout the day.

Architecture, as an art form and a functional discipline, has been significantly shaped by various cultural, societal, and individual influences throughout history, but the relationship between the Sun and men has left an indelible mark on the built environment. From ancient civilizations to modern times, either as a worship or a more functional use of the sunlight, the Sun played a pivotal role in shaping architectural styles, structures, and even the very fabric of our cities.

GUGGENHEIM BILBAO. ADOBE STOCK

Imposing structures, from ancient temples and monoliths to modern skyscrapers, displayed the omnipresence of the Sun along with the mastery of the architects. Channeling the power of the Sun is somehow a way for men to showcase their strength and their triumph over their environment, potentially making it a significant element of Solar Idealism.

DESCENDING ODIN'S THRONE

DESCENDING ODIN'S THRONE
ENLIGHTENMENT, POSTMODERNISM, AND SOLAR PHENOMENOLOGY AS A GROUNDWORK FOR MEANING
C.B. ROBERTSON

Hurtling through the Void

By all appearances, Western civilization is imploding.

We have seen escalating civil unrest over the last decade in the United States, and elsewhere – Canada, France, England. There is economic uncertainty, and fear of new technology. War and rumors of war, corruption, and whisperings of truly dark levels of depravity among the highest echelons of leadership, all seem to eat away at the legitimacy that supports our world.

Contrasted with the optimism that seemed to dominate the late 19th and early 20th century, things seem worse than ever. There is a sense of dread, that we "have peaked." There is a great foreboding, a sense of weakness and uncertainty that, historically, tends to invite assertive force – as the vacuum left in the aftermath of the French Revolution and its failed government invited Napoleon. If a great Civil War were to break out in America, it might be the most unsurprising and expected conflict in recent history[1].

---

1   According to various data from 2022, between 43% and 50% of Americans believe civil war is likely in the next decade.

But what makes this implosion so surreal is that it feels self-imposed. The threats of Russia and China during the Cold War, of Germany in WWII, and of Mexico, the Amerindian tribes, and the French in centuries prior – all of these were outside threats. Today the danger is a kind of self-hatred, an oikophobia, held not by a fringe few, but by the most educated and most powerful in our society.

We live in what has been called the "postmodern condition"[2]. Postmodernism is generally defined as a "skepticism towards all metanarratives," which has been usefully summarized as the belief that *everything is propaganda*. Explicit postmodern philosophy is prevalent in the academy, but is strong implicitly in culture beyond the walls of the universities. Dr. Jordan Peterson has familiarized much of the public with some of the more potent postmodern ideas. He has spoken, for instance, of Derrida and his deconstruction of text and language, and of Foucault, who argued broadly that "knowledge" is just an expression of power.

These ideas have been directionally weaponized in a particular, political direction, such that it has become common to hear their echoes in city hall meetings, legal arguments, public schools, and even in business, where political activists press their influence. One might borrow from Foucault, and presume that these ideas were crafted *for* such political movements; were nothing *but* expressions of these political aspirations. But if we step out of the postmodern frame, and try to understand this historically, we can see a breadth to the condition that extends beyond the university, and even beyond the political left, where much of postmodern thought originated.

Even libertarianism exists today within an essentially postmodern framework. "Leave me alone" has become the essential spirit of libertarianism. But in substance, "leave me alone" is merely a restatement of the philosophical question "who are you to judge?" It is an application of postmodern skepticism to all claims of authority.

Indeed, the very possibility of authority is challenged by Ludwig

---

2   Lyotard, Jean-Francois. *The Postmodern Condition*. 1979.

von Mises' praxeology – where voluntary trades are taken as "good" by definition. The question "who are you to judge?" becomes as unanswerable to the libertarian as it is to the progressive.

Both the libertarian and the radical might argue that this deconstruction of authority is in fact freeing to the individual. But as we have seen in the past several decades, these arguments have had the opposite effect. The problem is that arguments criticizing the judgment of authority are criticisms of humanity in general; suspicions of power are simply macroscopic foreshadowing of suspicion toward the individual. Postmodern critique of human authority paves the way to inhuman authority – governance by system, by algorithm – rather than to human freedom.

Nevertheless, there is some defensive necessity in this skepticism. When asked if she could define "woman," Jurist Ketanji Brown Jackson refused to answer, on the grounds that she was "not a biologist." On the surface, this refusal appears as judicious deference to authority, but we see the reality of the situation more clearly when we go to the domain of the relevant authority – on university campuses, even a professional biologist can get in hot water for making the mistake of giving a concrete answer about the biological foundations for sex[34], especially if they do not balance the biological facts with the social, anthropological, and political theories that purportedly work their way into the identity of "woman."

We mock and dismiss all positive positions because all positive positions can be mocked and dismissed. We feel a strange kind of compulsion to destroy what can be destroyed, in the world of ideas – *und das mit Recht; denn alles, was entsteht, ist wert, daß es zugrunde geht...*[5]

When pushed, we – right, left, and center – no longer fall back on the

---

3   Levine, Jon. "Maine university in uproar after professor insists there are only 2 sexes." New York Post. 8 Oct, 2022.
4   Piro and Namazi. "Longtime biology professor says public college fired him for teaching X and Y chromosomes determine biological sex." Fire. 28 June, 2023.
5   Goethe, Johann. *Faust.* "And rightly so; since everything created, in turn deserves to perish."

stories that once united us. From our grand vantage point, these stories appear insubstantial, even silly. All we have left is this defensive, postmodern skepticism – or else we too risk destruction, along with the myths that we might find ourselves attached to. To avoid dying with our illusions, it seems we must ourselves become disillusioned. And we are aided along the path of disillusionment by devices in our pockets that grant us access to more information than we can even comprehend.

Jack Donovan wrote about this as the *hliðskjálf dilemma*[6], which forces us to confront not merely one belief, but all systems of belief. We can see – as if from Odin's throne, high on the mountains – the whole world, and indeed, all of time. Yet seeing a given story in comparison to other places, other stories, we see the parochialism, the incompleteness, even the falsehood, of all the stories – of all the myths that oriented us in the world. From high enough, all personal perspectives look pathetic and stupid, and worthy of destruction.

Now, from this position of a God, we experience the world in the state described by Nietzsche as the "death of God":

> But how have we done this? [...] What did we do when we unchained the earth from its sun? Whither is it moving now? Whither are we moving now? Away from all suns? Are we not perpetually falling? Backward, sideward, forward, in all directions? Is there any up or down left? Are we not straying as through an infinite nothing? Do we not feel the breath of empty space?[7]

This essay attempts to trace the story of how we did this – how we arrived in a postmodern condition with a death not only of God, but of *truth* – and to provide a framework for how we might move out of this darkness.

In part 1, I will demonstrate how the pursuit of objectivity, reason, justice, and truth – indeed all of Western philosophy – was ultimately

---

6   Donovan, Jack. *Fire in the Dark*. 2021.
7   Nietzsche, Friedrich. *The Gay Science*. 1887.

driven by the desire to eradicate vengeance and the blood feud. We'll retrace the origins of these ideals through the wars of the 20th century, through the Age of Reason, all the way back to ancient Greece and the myths on which the objective of reason was built.

In part 2, we will explore the ways in which mathematics, language, and perception reveal the limitations of objectivity which prevent it from achieving its aims.

In part 3, I will offer an alternative foundation for Western philosophy in the form of Solar Phenomenology, which offers a new orientation toward the world, one which rejects philosophical idealism and objectivity in favor of our own subjective nature, and the knowledge that this subjectivity permits.

PART 1

The Birth of Postmodernism out of the Age of Reason

Our investigation into the origins of postmodernism begins in the 20th century.

The word "postmodernism" was coined[8] in 1979, but the postmodern sentiment of disillusionment and suspicion was born decisively in the aftermath of the Second World War. What we now call "World War I" was initially called "the Great War," and was imagined by many to be "the final war." There were hopes of greater international cooperation and unity, that the last shreds of petty nationalism might die in the trenches of the Somme.

But instead, it was swiftly followed by a second, equally terrible war, culminating in the use of the most destructive weaponry the world had ever seen. And WWII segued almost seamlessly into a "Cold War," which was itself anxiously experienced in light of the blinding memory of Hiroshima and Nagasaki.

To understand how a great war could cause such disillusionment, one has to understand what these thinkers were abandoning – the "modernism" which the war drove the "postmodernists" past.
What they tried to abandon was the project of the *Enlightenment*.

The Enlightenment is also called "the Age of Reason" because its essential spirit was a faith in the power of human reason. It is usually described as beginning with René Descartes' 1637 *Discourse on Method* because his skeptical approach to knowledge ultimately picked up the entire edifice of human knowledge and moved it from the old foundation of myth to a new foundation of reason.

---

8   Here, postmodernism refers to philosophical postmodernism. Literary and artistic postmodernism of various genres existed much earlier in the 20th century, but that does not concern this essay.

Descartes' declaration *cogito ergo sum*[9] remains one of the most profound pronouncements in Western philosophy, not because of what it *says* but because of what it *does*. Coming from a world that had God at its center, Descartes shifted the foundation. Through a systematic distrust of the senses, the pursuit of certainty turned inward, and the reasoning mind of the individual became the bedrock – 'perhaps I am being deceived, but I know there is at least an *I* that is being deceived.' He believed he had found certainty in a hurricane of uncertainty, and used this point of certainty as the launching point for all further investigations. He retained God, but God was now grounded in reason, rather than reason being grounded in God.

Descartes' *Discourse* in the 17th century marks the conventional beginning of the Enlightenment, but his line of thinking was well received in no small part thanks to 200 years of priming. The Renaissance of the preceding centuries had seen the gradual reintroduction of Greek language and texts into European culture. This revival expressed itself in art and in architecture, and also in philosophy. And indeed, we find even Descartes' famous idea – grounding even the Gods in reason – in seedling form within the Platonic dialogue of *Euthyphro*. There, Socrates asks whether the Gods love something because it is good, or if something is good because it is loved by the Gods. Merely asking the question seems to shift the foundation, subjecting the Gods to human judgment, rather than viewing the Gods as the standard against which judgment is made. It is unclear whether Descartes was directly influenced by the Greeks; it is more clear that the rest of Europe *was* inspired by this rediscovered world of thought and literature.

It is not an exaggeration then to say that the Age of Reason originated not with Descartes, but with Socrates. The recovery of the writings of the Greeks provided a backdrop, if not a direct influence, for a resurgence in interest in the pursuit of reason and objectivity. Even the radical skepticism and doubt which characterized Descartes' *Discourse* mirrored the doubt and skepticism that drove

---

9   "I think therefore I am."

Socrates in his questioning of the people of Athens.

So postmodernism emerged after the second World War in the 1940s, as an expression of profound disillusionment with Age of Reason. The Age of Reason grew out of the 17th century, as a culmination of a revival of Greek ideas that had taken root back in the 4th century BC. This "Enlightenment" was characterized by a faith in the salvific power of reason.

So, again, we must ask: why did a war destroy this faith in reason? What does conflict have to do with truth?

Peace, Justice, and the Spell of Aeschylus

To understand the significance of WWII to the Enlightenment faith in reason, let us explore the "reason" of the Greeks that Europe had uncovered as a prelude to this Age of Reason.

It is no exaggeration to say that European culture is a blood-descendant of Greek culture. Even before the discovery of Homeric texts, Achilles and Hector were well-known characters in European folklore – Hector was, in fact, the first of the "Nine Worthies" that set the example for all European chivalry. The Biblical New Testament was recorded in Greek, making the Greek language as much the linguistic home of Christianity as Golgotha or Bethlehem might be its geographic home. The medieval scholastic monk Thomas Aquinas drew inspiration from the Greek philosopher Aristotle, while the 4th century Augustine of Hippo was a strong Platonist. Even the theological debates at the highest levels of European Christendom were iterations of debates between pre-Christian Greeks.

But all Greeks lived in the shadow of Homer, of Homer's *Iliad* in particular, which was treated much in the way the Bible was treated in Christian Europe. It was Homer who united the Greeks *as Greeks*, who gave them a shared vision of themselves in brilliant fragments of poetry and high aspirations.

Homer's epic tale of the Trojan war created the personalities of the Gods and of the heroes by which Greece knew itself. It made Troy the chronological and spiritual anchor of notions of good and evil, piety and pollution, beauty and ugliness. And upon this Homeric narrative foundation, another playwright fashioned the myth and the direct prescription that ultimately became the Enlightenment. That playwright was Aeschylus.

Aeschylus' most famous series of plays was a trilogy called the Oresteia. Comprised of *Agamemnon*, *The Libation Bearers*, and *Eumenides*, the trilogy depicts the conclusion of the horrific intrafamilial blood-feud of the House of Atreus. It begins with Agamemnon's return to Mycenae after the conclusion of the Trojan War, whereupon he is killed by his own wife, Clytemnestra, and her lover, Aegisthus. After Clytemnestra kills Agamemnon, their son Orestes (for whom the Trilogy is named) kills his mother. Clytemnestra's ghost then summons the spirits of the *Erinyes* – the "Furies" – to pursue her son Orestes and seek vengeance.

Just as the Furies are about to overtake Orestes, he takes refuge in a temple of Apollo, and Athena intervenes. Athena persuades the Furies to curb their vengeance and accept "real justice" by putting Orestes on trial for matricide instead. The trial eventually delivers a 7-6 "not guilty" verdict, and while the Furies are not happy about the outcome, they accept the verdict, and are transformed into *Eumenides* – "those of good intentions." In this way, the blood feud was resolved.

It cannot be overemphasized how profoundly Aeschylus is legitimized by Homer himself, in the way that the themes of Aeschylus are mirrored in Homer's epics. At the end of Homer's *Odyssey*, we see Athena intervene in a manner similar to *Eumenides*: after Odysseus and his son Telemachus kill the suitors that had been courting Penelope, the families of some of the men arm up to seek vengeance against Odysseus. They are about to fight when Athena appears and calls the conflict to a close.

In the *Iliad*, we find the most poetic effort and power put into the creation of Achilles' shield. Over the course of 129 lines, this description includes, among other things, the following depiction of Hephaestus' handiwork:

> *On it he wrought in all their beauty two cities of mortal men [...] The people were assembled in the market place, where a quarrel had arisen, and two men were disputing over the blood price for a man who had been killed. One man promised full restitution in a public statement, but the other refused and would accept nothing. Both then made for an arbiter, to have a decision; and people were speaking up on either side, to help both men. But the heralds kept the people in hand, as meanwhile the elders were in session on benches of polished stone in the sacred circle and held in their hands the staves of the heralds who lift their voices. The two men rushed before these, and took turns speaking their cases, and between them lay on the ground two talents of gold, to be given to that judge who in this case spoke the straightest [díkēn] opinion.*[10]

This passage depicts – in the dreamlike form of a craftsman's art on a shield – the very first trial by jury. It describes "justice" in terms of *dike* ($\delta i \kappa \eta \nu$), which Lattimore translates as "straight(est)", which is compatible with, yet nonetheless different from, the Furies' notion of *justice as vengeance*.

Greg Nagy defines *dike* as "justice," or "judgment," and in some contexts means "straight":

> *We see at work here a metaphor that pervades the Hesiodic Works and Days: dikē or 'justice' is straight and direct or unidirectional, whereas hubris as the opposite of justice is crooked and indirect or multidirectional. The etymology of the noun dikē, derived from the verb deik-nunai, which means 'to point' or 'to indicate,' shows the built-in idea of direction, directness, directedness.*[11]

---

10   Homer, *Iliad.* 18.490-508
11   Nagy, Gregory. *The Ancient Greek Hero in 24 Hours.* 2013.

It is notable for our common understanding of "justice" that the opposite of *dike* is *hubris*, a word which has maintained its moral connotations into English over 2,800 years. *Hubris* is arrogance, and an outrage against the Gods, but in its original meaning, implied an *excess*, in direction or even growth. While *dike* is not identical with moderation, it is fair to say that moderation is also an opposite of *hubris*.

But this notion of "justice" is not the same as that held by the ancient Furies. To the Furies, vengeance *is* justice. Even the *Iliad* carries this idea in its first word. "Mênis" is usually translated as "anger" or "wrath" or "rage," but is a much heavier word in ancient Greek than any English translation can convey. Leonard Muellner defines mênis as "an irrevocable cosmic sanction that prohibits some from taking their superiors for equals and others from taking their equals for inferiors"[12]. This sanction carried indiscriminate, collateral damage as retribution not only against the guilty, but against everyone. The enforcement of justice was vengeance, no matter the cost: *fiat justitia, ruat caelum*[13].

Or, as Nietzsche puts it more simply, "*what justice means to us is precisely that the world be filled with the storms of our revenge*"[14].

What Aeschylus does in the *Oresteia* is remarkable: he creates a new purpose of justice: *to end the blood feud.*[15] The aim of this 'new justice' is not the repayment of debts, but peace. To Aeschylus, *Dike* becomes something like "moderation" – "justice" in the sense Plato meant in *The Republic*, where it was written *dikaiosýne* – which was

---

12   Muellner, Leonard. *The Anger of Achilles: Mênis in Greek Epic.* 1996.
13   "Do justice, and let the heavens fall."
14   Nietzsche, Friedrich. *Thus Spake Zarathustra.* 1883. "Das gerade heisse uns Gerechtigkeit, dass die Welt voll werde von den Unwettern unsrer Rache." It is critical to note that Nietzsche himself is not advocating this position, but distilling the idea as the position of the tarantula, and something to reject in absolute terms.
15   It is impossible to know for certain whether Aeschelus in fact *created* this notion of justice or merely described a view that preceded him, and was held in his time; but for our purposes, his stories lent mythological credence to the idea. As a matter of functional history, the *Oresteia* legitimized this new conception of justice, which is more relevant to the question of the trajectory of the Age of Reason than creating it.

not a connotation that 'justice' had carried before. Such a notion was certainly not embodied in the vengeful Furies – there, *dike* carried only its direct meaning of "straightforward." "An eye for an eye" is nothing if not direct.

But this new justice of *Eumenides* was not about repayment at all. It was rather a kind of disposition, adopted as a means toward an end: namely, *civilization*. People could only live side-by-side in harmony if the blood feud was put to an end, and direct vengeance was transcended, delegated upward to a higher authority – be it Athena or the State or 'God' or 'reason' – or abandoned entirely. And with this new understanding, "justice" of the old kind (vengeance) became *injustice* – excess and malice, at odds with the Aeschelian spirit of justice.

Justice, in other words, becomes about being 'one of good intentions' – *eumenides*. We see this ideal embodied in Plato's Socrates, who argues in *The Republic* that the just man is only just insofar as he does good to others, and it is not right to injure even those who do wrong to you:

> Then if someone asserts that it's just [*díkaion*] to give what is owed to each man–and he understands by this that injury is owed to enemies by the just man [*dikaíou ándrós*] and help to friends–the man who said it was not wise. For he wasn't telling the truth [*alethẽ*]. For it has become apparent to us that it is never just [*díkaion*] to injure anyone.[16]

Plato is notorious for advancing all varieties of arguments, many which contradict each other, and without any clear indication of which Plato himself holds. Nevertheless, the ideal of "he with good intentions" as the just man was certainly a view held by many of his day, including his instructor, Socrates. Such was Socrates' respect for the state and the authorities and his fellow citizens that he did not resist their persecution, nor did he even flee death when presented with the opportunity. His compulsion to philosophize, even at the

---

16   Plato, *Republic*. 335e.

cost of his own life, was built upon the conviction that his efforts were a service to his city.

According to this view, if Socrates is wiser, more "reasonable" than others, it is not necessarily by virtue of his intellect, but rather by his good and peaceful intentions. He rejects malice and vengeance, even against enemies like Meletus, his primary accuser.

When Socrates is elevated as the patron saint of modern rationalism and the highest moral ideal of the scientist and the patriotic citizen, he simultaneously becomes the standard of rationality and reason itself. To be just is to be reasonable, which is why even to this day, the *reasonable person* standard carries such weight in court and in the minds of the public when judging the moral culpability of a fellow citizen in a dispute. The standard is, in fact, definitional: the reasonable man is a just man, and the just man is a reasonable man. And, of course, to be just requires having good intentions.

What we end up with is a *civilizational formula*, a recipe for peaceful coexistence and the possibility of long-term investment in society with the hopes of the preservation and accumulation of a growing legacy. This civilizational formula is built upon the magical transformation of justice from "vengeance" into "good intentions." With the transformation of justice came the idealization of reason and rationality, first set forth explicitly by Plato in *Euthyphro*, but which re-emerged during the Age of Reason with Renes Descartes. What the Age of Reason symbolized was the return of hope in the possibility of civilization based upon reason and rationality; that truth – or the pursuit of truth – could unite mankind against the horror of the Furies in their true form: revenge.

A modern audience is likely unfamiliar with this horror. We have this civilizational formula to thank for our unfamiliarity, and we really *should* be grateful, given the kind of world our ancestors likely lived through:

> ...but where do we look when we are no longer led and protected by

the hand of Homer, striding back into the pre-Homeric world? Only into the night and horror, into the products of an imagination accustomed to the horrible. What kind of earthly existence is reflected in these repulsively terrible theogonic myths: a life over which alone the children of the Night rule, Strife, Lustful Greed, Deception, Old Age, and Death.[17]

But gratitude aside, what is essential to recognize is that this civilizational formula requires the rejection of myth... or, at least, the subjugation of myth beneath reason. Sacred stories, as illustrated by *Euthyphro*[18], can be contradictory, unhelpful (or worse) in resolving disputes like that between Euthyphro and his father. Only cold reason can intervene like gray-eyed Athena and resolve disputes in a manner that feels sufficiently objective as to assuage the Furies. So myth must submit to reason. According to the Socrates of Plato's *Republic*, we must be willing to censor the stories of Homer's Olympus. And for Descartes, even God must be justified by reason. Yet, as should be clear, this Enlightenment formula is also itself *built upon myth* – namely, the ideal depicted in Achilles' shield, and then brought into being by the spell of Aeschylus.

Our world has been the world governed by this civilizational formula, up until the middle of the 20th century.

Mutually Assured Destruction and the Postmodern Conundrum

Let us return from classical Greece to the last century.

The decades after WWII saw much skeptical speculation about the limitations of reason. The Germans were, prior to the war, looked

---

17   Nietzsche, Friedrich. "Homer's Contest." 1872.

18   In Euthyphro, Socrates questions a young man named Euthyphro about the nature of piety. Euthyphro is taking his own father to court for murdering a slave, and he believes piety is following the will of the Gods. Among his questions, Socrates points out that the Gods are often at odds with each other, and which both makes Euthyphro's definition of piety unhelpful at times, and also brings into question the relationship between piety and the Gods.

upon by much of the world as leaders in the domain of reason, not only for their technological, industrial, and organizational superiority, but also because of their accomplishments in art, literature, and especially philosophy. Indeed, the philosophy of the 18th, 19th, and early 20th century were dominated by Kant, Hegel, Schoppenhauer, and Nietzsche, as well as Husserl and Heidegger, who we will return to later. Yet these heights of reason and thought did not stop them from holding on to the grudges from the first World War, nor did it prevent them from invading Poland in 1939 (and worse).

The problem was not the Germans *per se*. The problem was all of humanity, as demonstrated by the Germans.

The end of the war brought no relief either. The presence of nuclear weapons had changed things. After the destruction of Hiroshima and Nagasaki, the threat of total annihilation hung over the world like a radioactive sword of Damocles, and over Russia and the United States in particular.

The solution to the problem of nuclear weapons was found in mathematics – specifically from game theory – in the concept of *mutually assured destruction*, or "M.A.D." The idea is that if the threat of annihilation is matched with reciprocity – "if you kill us, we'll kill you too" – then paradoxically all of the killing will (hopefully) be avoided... at least, so long as the threat is believable. It was a philosophy of deterrence taken to its final conclusion and test.
So far, it seems to have worked[19].

---

19   There are critics who point out near-misses and accidents as a kind of argument that luck was what carried the USSR and USA through the end of the Cold War without a nuclear bombing, and that mutually assured destruction had little to do with this success – was, if anything, an exacerbation of the risk. But for all the technical failures and false-signs of missiles, neither side actually launched a missile because there was no evidence of a detonation. Reciprocity begins with a response to a strike, not merely a signal, and the technical failures can be read as much in favor of mutually assured destruction as against it, since merely the posturing of the kind seen in the Cuban Missile Crisis could have been a cause for preemptive war in previous eras. Indeed, it has been argued that Hitler's invasion of the Soviet Union was just such a preemptive strike meant to anticipate an attack he believed was coming from Stalin, but which had not happened yet (Ellis, Frank. *Barbarossa 1941*. 2015).

But however logical mutually assured destruction may seem, it runs afoul of the fundamental principle of *reasonability* according to the Enlightenment sense of the term. One who engages in the strategy of mutually assured destruction does so with the promise of violence. This cuts against the good intentions of the Socratic "just man" who, like a doctor, *does no harm*. Mutually assured destruction reveals the illusion that undergirds the Enlightenment: reason is not the same as justice, and neither are identical with good intentions. The success of deterrence eviscerates the spell of Aeschylus.

But the problem with the Age of Reason goes further.

In their *The Dialectic of Enlightenment*, published at the very end of the second World War, Max Horkheimer and Theodore Adorno expressed pessimism over the possibility of the project of the Enlightenment. After defining "Enlightenment" as the escape from fear and the accomplishment of human mastery over nature, they observe that the earth is "radiant with triumphant calamity," despite the proliferation of the project of Enlightenment. Enlightenment sought to "dispel myths, to overthrow fantasy with knowledge," but as they wrote:

> *Mythology itself set in motion the endless process of enlightenment by which, with ineluctable necessity, every definite theoretical view is subjected to the annihilating criticism that it is only a belief, until even the concepts of mind, truth, and indeed, enlightenment itself have been reduced to animistic magic.*[20]

Indeed, Horkheimer and Adorno claim that "Enlightenment is mythical fear radicalized." Rationality replaced the fear of the blood feud with the fear *of the fear* of the blood feud. The Age of Reason did not escape the mystification of myth; it only created the illusion of the escape from illusion. The complete disillusionment required of a truly Enlightened, objective frame would require destroying the very myth which spurred the Age of Reason.

---

20   Horkheimer and Adorno, *The Dialectic of Enlightenment*. 1947.

Along with this illusion of the escape from myth came the illusion of the escape from the violence -- specifically, the cycles of violence that characterized pastoral honor-cultures. The axe of the blood-feud was buried, but it was replaced with the industrial violence of global wars between nation-states. This escalation of violence was, in fact, the logical consequence of delegating authority for vengeance upward.

The delegation required by Athena to banish personal revenge and make civilization possible also concentrated power, but higher authorities are not immune from the excesses that once motivated personal vengeance. Without a possibility of recourse, the delegation of authority made brutal tyranny not only possible, but *justified*, and also exacerbated the risk of wars between nation-states.

A personal vendetta may involve two families, maybe even their extended families. In some cases it might even include a whole village. But war undertaken by a nation-state may conscript and kill men from across entire empires, without any personal interest at all from the soldiers themselves. This was the lament of Achilles when he was conscripted into the war against Troy based upon a broad wedding oath among the Greeks:

> I for my part did not come here for the sake of the Trojan spearmen to fight against them, since to me they have done nothing. Never yet have they driven away my cattle or my horses, never in Phthia where the soil is rich and men grow great did they spoil my harvest, since indeed there is much that lies between us, the shadowy mountains and the echoing sea; but for your sake, O great shamelessness, we followed...[21]

In the honor-cultures of pre-Homeric life, where justice was simply "vengeance," revenge was viewed as a right and even a duty. But it could just as easily be thought of in game-theoretical terms. Math is not required to understand the principle, but the math of Cold War brinkmanship reiterated timeless wisdom: when wrong is

---

21   Homer, *Iliad*. 1.152-158.

reciprocated, it deters wrong in the future. When it is understood that a man will kill the man who injures his family, it makes potential wrong-doers think twice. Perhaps the reason vengeance was personified in terrifying, pre-Olympian deities like the Furies was because vengeance works, and was known to work since before the Greeks knew the classical pantheon.

The logic of mutually assured destruction in the post-WWII age brought society back into a feeling of pre-civilized posturing in violence, overtures to ill-intentions and recklessness, even questionable sanity. As Horkheimer and Adorno describe it, it is as if Enlightenment gave way not to a "truly human" mode of existence, but to a "new kind of barbarism."

But this barbarism is simply the coldness of the objectivity sought for by Enlightenment. The good intentions that were associated with peace among individuals turned out to be counterproductive to the project of peace at scale: indeed, reason itself split good intentions from peace.

But perhaps most importantly of all, this divergence itself revealed the aim of peace to be subjective, not objective. And so the Age of Reason has had to fall back upon its final redoubt: numbers.

PART 2

Machina Ex Dei

Today we find ourselves in the administrative society – a society increasingly governed by systems and by numbers. Statistics and graphs have become the benchmark of persuasive argumentation and the sure sign of a best practice. Anything with "data" supporting it is, at the very least, is granted a degree of leniency when in error – leniency which is not extended to those who err in their own, less numerically-justified judgment.

But in truth, our focus on quantitative metrics is a culmination of the idealization of reason and objectivity. Numbers are pure. As Adorno and Horkheimer wrote:

> The mythologizing equation of Forms with numbers in Plato's last writings expresses the longing of all demythologizing: number becomes the enlightenment's canon [...] It makes dissimilar things comparable by reducing them to abstract quantities. For the Enlightenment, anything which cannot be resolved into numbers, and ultimately into one, is illusion; modern positivism consigns it to poetry. Unity remains the watchword from Parmenides to Russell. All gods and qualities must be destroyed.[22]

The imperative of the Enlightenment is objectivity because only by objectivity can disputes be resolved in a binding fashion. Through a sufficiently objective lens, all becomes one and a principle for direction in the resolution of conflicts emerges. The objectivity of a judge can be (and has been) challenged. But in its purity, mathematics seems beyond the reach of subjective bias, which was the aim of the Age of Reason. Numbers and impartial *systems* hold the hope of true objectivity... and, indeed, *truth*.

---

22   Horkheimer and Adorno, *The Dialectic of Enlightenment.*

Yet the nature of numbers is somewhat misunderstood. Far from an ideal of objectivity, numbers have been the object of mystical interest since the days of Pythagoras, if not further. And there is reason to doubt their objectivity, beyond the mere abuse of statistics and the gentle gaslighting of supposedly objective algorithmic manipulation on social media platforms today.

Let us consider numbers in themselves.

The number "five" does not exist in nature.

It is an abstraction of an idea, a quantity that is relative to another discrete quantity. We identify a single apple as "one," and only by this assumption do five fruits from an apple tree constitute "five." The statement "an apple is one" is a premise, but it is not "true" in any objective sense. It is an assertion of identity that is arbitrarily presumed for the sake of convenience. If apples were quantified by weight, rather than by discrete fruits, a completely separate system of quantification could be imagined. Arithmetic done in base-15 is just as valid as arithmetic done in base-10, or base-2. Non-Euclidean geometry is just as valid as Euclidean geometry. They only have different assumptions.

With this in mind, it is clear that mathematics is actually only objective so long as one's assumptions are objective. The use of mathematics in argumentation today is largely the art of hiding the subjective biases of these assumptions, but this too is being pushed back on, even from within mathematics itself. Gödel's famous incompleteness theorem demonstrated – mathematically – that a mathematical system cannot prove or justify its own initial assumptions, thus all mathematical systems are "incomplete."

But we did not need mathematics to know this. We could understand this simply through language, and the recognition that *mathematics is just a derivative of language*. It is, in fact, language purged of all discrete subject matter; a pure grammar.

This can be understood when we think about the purpose and application of mathematics. Mathematical identities (like "5") are not even representations of "things," but representations of ideas or categories. These identities are the linguistic representation of a "form" which permits mathematics to be universal, and to apply across all languages (like grammars). But the representative nature is the same as it is with language proper. Mathematics has simply reduced this representative substitution to the minimum signs necessary for logical evaluation.

It is easily understood that all mathematical statements can be rewritten in conventional language, but it is equally true that all conventional linguistic sentences can be re-written into mathematical statements (so long as the sentence is grammatical). There is no difference in form (grammar) between "$p = q$" and "all men are mortal." The former is, in fact, the purely grammatical representation of the latter – *the mathematicalization* of a linguistic sentence. All that has happened is the words of the sentence have been replaced with mathematical symbols representing the grammatical category. One must only accept a loss of semantic precision as the discrete representative words are replaced with stand-in categories such as x or y, and the nature of mathematics as pure grammar comes into focus. One knows less of the substance that is meaningful to humans when "all men are mortal" is re-written as "$p = q$," but the translation is correct.

Because these categories are grammatically universal, they often seem more "objective" and true than mere words. It can feel as if our construction of mathematical formulas are not constructions but "discoveries," as if $a^2 + b^2 = c^2$ existed in the universe prior to mankind. But this is not true, because as with numbers like "five," our formula is not identical with the relationship it represents. Indeed, even the triangle which $a^2 + b^2 = c^2$ describes does not exist in the world. It is delineated by us, arbitrated into existence when we say "let us call these three points a 'triangle'." And $a^2 + b^2 = c^2$ helpfully tells us about the relationship between the arbitrary sides created by these arbitrary points. The relationship existed before our mathematical description of it, but the triangle itself did not. With this in mind, the notion that we "discover" these mathematical principles becomes circular. We only feel like we "discover" mathematical formulas, rather than create them, when we confuse our own mathematical presuppositions and axioms with objective reality, or confuse the letters on a piece of paper with the world we are attempting to model.

If our presuppositions correspond closely to reality, then the mathematics we derive from these systems can be extremely useful -- but the pure objectivity that we strive for in the world of mathematics can never give us these presuppositions.

And the purity of these categories and formulas collapse back into subjectivity again the moment they are translated into the real world – when "five" becomes "five apples."

All acts of quantification require the exclusion of variables. A nation's GDP, for instance, implies an equation of national health with the movement of money. Economists will say that, of course, GDP does not *really* measure national health, only the movement of money... but the reason it is brought up in the first place is because the movement of money is treated as though it were a kind of heuristic for national health. The particular operational definition of a term is strategically swapped with the sense in which it is used in actual application – when it is spoken about with weight, as though it *mattered in the physical world* – as though these two senses were the same.

Economists will generally agree that the nation is economically healthy when the GDP is up, and only retreat to the technical meaning (with its merely technical significance) when the equivocation is pointed out: '*Yes, psychological health is down, addiction and suicide are up, divorce is up, general satisfaction is down, employment is down, civil unrest is at a 150-year high... GDP is just one metric.*'

All quantifications are like this. This is not to say that quantitative analysis cannot be useful – the game theory behind mutually assured destruction has worked quite well. It only means that quantitative analysis can never be sufficient in understanding a field, because the conversion of things into numbers is a reduction, and one cannot know *in advance* the significance of what is erased for the sake of clear, mathematical simplicity.

The systems we have created – increasingly governed by computer algorithms – suffer a similar problem: they can never be complete. And subjective bias often hides in the forgotten, incomplete assumptions.

Mathematics still holds a kind of mystical enchantment over much of the world, and systems built upon mathematical principles govern much of our society today. The logic of the Enlightenment requires it.

Since Aeschylus' transformation of 'justice,' we have created a machine, as impersonal as possible, for the purpose of finding an arbiter of sufficient objectivity to govern our society and maintain peace. This machine kills gods. It has left us in a state of godlessness, floating in the void with our numbers... only to discover that the numbers are not as objective as we had believed – that they are not a path to truth because the assumptions required by these numbers are not relevant, not sufficiently precise, or else the assumption-makers are as biased as the rest of the humans whose subjective judgment we sought to escape.

Our faith in mathematics and the power of numbers has not yet been shattered. But it is only a matter of time before enough sophisticated mathematical models fail – perhaps in the domains of economics, medicine, and climate science – before faith in models generally collapses. Then the persuasive power of number, as a benchmark for objective and unchallengeable truth, will also fall.

"Truth" and the Problem of Language

The appeal of mathematics stems from conflating universality with truth. When the subjective axioms are forgotten, one can sometimes experience a kind of dizzying, mystical experience in mathematics, as though one is glimpsing Truth itself.

But as we have seen, the universality in mathematics is contingent upon axioms which are themselves not mathematically derived, as well as the more menial and equally non-mathematical translation back and forth between the world of matter and the world of numbers. Both the delineation of axioms and this process of translation fall into the domain of language.

Even seemingly invincible axioms, such as "$1 = 1$," must retreat into the murky waters of language if anyone asks "...and what is 1?" Tautologies are only tautological by definition, and may not be practically useful or even descriptive of reality beyond a wand-waving "let us assume..."

In short, mathematics is both a derivative *of* language, and ultimately only valid in application contingent *upon* language.

So where does this leave us in the pursuit of objective truth?

The trouble with language as a mechanism for the pursuit of truth is that language is representative. As with the initial axioms of mathematics, the value of language only extends as far as a word corresponds with the thing it is representing – "chair" accurately conveying the object one might happen to be sitting in. But because these verbal (or written) representations are agreed upon and arbitrary[23], they are not universal, in connotation or even denotation.

---

23   We can see the arbitrariness in language even in the use of onomatopoeia animal sounds across languages: the sound of a chicken might be represented as "cluck cluck" or "bawk bawk" in America, or as "pio pio" in Spain. No particular verbal expression is more or less "correct" in this representative manner, despite their initially representative origins, and the chicken did not tell us how to write its own sound.

Words are not – and cannot be – truly objective.

This brings up a question even below the suspicion of the objectivity of mathematics. Reason, good intentions, and objectivity all point toward this notion of "truth," a word we have referenced but which has not been defined. We are entitled to ask with Pontius Pilate (of one who claimed to testify to the Truth) "*ti estin alētheia?*"[24]

What is 'truth?'

Aristotle argued that "truth" is not a description of existence, but a description of language[25]. We can understand this by thinking about the antithesis: "false." Speaking of what is "false" only makes sense in the context of describing something that someone has said, but which does not correspond with what exists. A rock which does not exist isn't "false." That which is not, simply isn't. No word is necessary. The same is the case with "truth." A description of reality does not require an affirmation of itself. There is no semantic difference between a man saying "there is a blue rock on the ground" and another man saying "it is the truth that there is a blue rock on the ground," except that we might assume that the second man is concurring with the first. "Truth" does not describe reality, but words.

As a form of "meta-language," the notion of "truth" becomes tricky. Since many things are – and many things are said about what is – "the truth" takes on an association with an impossibly broad collection of things. Yet "truth" is still conceptualized as something separate from the discrete statements to which it might be applied. It has grown into a thing in itself, perhaps a quality other things which exist possess, or perhaps even the necessary quality for the possibility of existence! (This would be a strange and grand feature for a word used to describe other words).

---

24   John 18:38.
25   "To say that what is is not, or that what is not is, is false; but to say that what is is, and what is not is not, is true; and therefore also he who says that a thing is or is not will say either what is true or what is false. But neither what is nor what is not is said not to be or to be." Aristotle. *Metaphysics*. Book 4. 1011b.25.

We have looked at the association between justice and *dike*, but "truth" has its own Greek words – most notably *noúmenon* and *aletheia*.

Let us explore the *noumenon*.

In juxtaposition with *phenomenon*, which refers to an object as it appears through the senses (from the Greek *phainómenon* - "that which appears"), the "noumenon" refers to a thing as it exists, apart from the senses – the *ding an sich*[26] according to Kant.

Kant argued that usually, knowledge begins with experience[27]. Specifically, knowledge is acquired through our senses; we perceive the *thing in itself* as a *phenomenon*, which is the appearance of the thing, but not the "true" thing. Since we can only know the phenomenon of a thing, we can never know for certain how closely the phenomenon matches the noumenon.

But Kant was not a skeptic. He believed it was possible to acquire what he called *a priori* knowledge ("prior to experience"). Such "pure" knowledge does not depend upon the senses, instead deriving true knowledge and the possibility of certainty by means of analysis and synthesis of identities and necessities. In philosophy, this approach is sometimes called *transcendentalism*, and has given rise to "transcendental arguments" which attempt to show that something is a necessary condition of something else. Kant's famous categorical imperative – "act only according to that maxim whereby you can at the same time will that it should become a universal law" – is in fact an *a priori* synthesis of what objective moral law must be, based upon the nature of morality itself. The assumption, of course, is that morality isn't *really* morality unless it is universal.

But in all possibilities of *a priori* knowledge, language is required to reach some conclusion. Language is in fact the mediating mechanism of thought, and the words that comprise language are not *a*

26　　　　"Thing in itself."
27　　　　Kant, Immanuel, *The Critique of Pure Reason*. 1781.

priori knowledge. Even Descartes' famous ontological argument for *a priori* knowledge of the triangle[28] requires the language of mathematics in order to conceive of the relationship at all, since thought on abstract subjects like this requires language in order to make inferences or deductions. Identities required for analysis are inherently linguistic. And language – logical, mathematical or conventional – comes from experience[29].

Kant's transcendental principle of necessity destroys transcendentalism with the linguistic requirement of experience. "Truth" is not accessible by *a priori* analysis, and for this reason, we also cannot come to understand what truth *is* by transcendental logic.

We get much closer to the noumenon by looking at the language directly. "Noumenon" is a conjugation of the Greek *noōs*, meaning "mind." Contra-Kant, these "mental conceptions" or "mental apprehensions" do not describe objective "things in themselves," but the subjective impressions and ideas of subjective beings. The very idea of the noumenon is a byproduct of language and experience.

But what of our other word, *aletheia*? Indeed, if we go back to when Socrates speaks of "telling the truth," as he was quoted earlier, he speaks of álethē.

Aletheia translates literally as "not concealed" or "un-concealed," and can be colloquially understood as what is "uncovered" or "revealed." There is a connotation to aletheia as something rare and unseen by the public, that goes all the way back to Parmenides:

> *Meet it is that thou shouldst learn all things, as well the unshaken heart of persuasive truth [Àletheíes], as the opinions [dóx-*

---

28   Descartes argued that it can be known based on reason alone (*a priori*) that the inside angles of a triangle add up to 180°, and that this fact is not a part of the definition of a triangle as three points in space, but something derived from it.

29   Noam Chomsky has argued for a "universal grammar," which might be misunderstood to imply that grammar is, itself, universal. Chomsky's theory holds that the capacity to find grammatical rules is inborn and universal in human beings. But grammatical structure still varies around the world, and language requires semantic axioms for the application of grammar.

as] of mortals in which is no true [ouk ... álethes] belief at all.[30]
This connotation carries its way through Socrates and Jesus
forward all the way to the philosophy of the modern age, where
"the truth" is something that carries the mystique of an ancient
scroll. Conspiracy theorists are mocked for their unfalsifiable
notions of "what really happened," but perhaps when they speak
of "the truth," they are more closely matching the spirit of the
word than even scientists. This is not to say that conspiracy the-
orists are factual or correct, only that they are capturing a tone
in the original use of the word "truth," as something hidden in
the dark, remote and unknown to the masses who possess only
"opinion."

The elites who dominate our academic and governing institutions,
though they usually disagree with conspiracy theorists for a variety
of aesthetic and epistemological reasons, are not so different from
conspiracy theorists in their belief that "the truth" is something rare,
which they possess and which the masses (*especially* conspiracy
theorists) do not. It is something uncovered only by a few, and of
which there is none at all to be found in the opinions of the public.

What elites and conspiracy theorists demonstrate is a bottomless
well beneath the word "truth." There is always something hidden
beneath the thing uncovered, in part because language – like math-
ematics – is necessarily incomplete:

> *The tao that can be told*
>
> *is not the eternal Tao* [31]

As a translation of *aletheia*, the very word "truth" has colored our re-
lationship to it, and biased our search for the objective in favor of
the rare. But objectivity has – by definition – no preferences. Insofar
as truth is objective, it would not matter whether it was to be found
commonly among the crowds or hidden away with monks in the
mountains.

---

30   Parmenides, *On Nature.*
31   Lao Tzu. *Tao Te Ching.*

Of course, objective truth must be something rare indeed among people, since humans are subjective by nature. Our very existence is at odds with objectivity; how then could truth be found among us? On a more practical level, the reason that truth was elevated in the first place was to arbitrate disputes. Judgment (*dike*) only binds the Furies when it is believed to be objective, and the illusion of objectivity can only be maintained when those who speak on behalf of Truth remain distant, mysterious and inscrutable – even unreachable. If "truth" was close at hand to the masses, what authority would it wield in maintaining peace? If everyone already possessed universal truth, there would be no disputes; if there were disputes and the spokesmen for arbitrating Truth and Justice were seen to be like the common folk, possessing no greater knowledge or wisdom, they would lose the lofty grandeur required of their role. Seen up close, the public might doubt their wisdom and make up their own decisions – their own judgments. "Truth" must be rare for practical reasons.

And does "truth" itself not carry a connotative tone – as all words do? It has a subjective quality that falls short of its own objective ideal. A subjective medium like language is incapable of bearing or conveying anything in a truly objective manner, since our subjective biases and associations are the very mechanism by which language conveys information from speaker to receiver.

Understanding the nature and trickiness of language truly is key. The entirety of this convoluted web only exists because of an equivocation between "truth" as a descriptor (i.e., "it is true that some cats are black") and "Truth" as an abstract idea (i.e., "the Truth shall set you free"). When one considers these two senses of the term, there is in fact no overlap in meaning between the two. What is implied in the breadth and depth of "The Truth" is completely different – in meaning and tone – from anything that could be described in a discrete, true statement. Even a commitment to tell discrete, true statements (or at least not tell false ones) falls short of the full meaning of the grand Truth, since true statements can be misleading, and in any case cannot convey the *full truth*. Conversely, it is sometimes possible to convey something true by means of fiction.

The mechanism of illusion has been to define Truth as a foundation for the possibility of discreet truths, as if the two were related. Truth is then asserted to be identifiable through coherence and internal consistency, according to certain presupposed axioms (perhaps one of these axioms is Truth itself). These axioms serve as the mooring threads, and from there, the rest of the linguistic spider's web eventually spins itself. But for all that sticky thread, "true" is still just a linguistic category for distinguishing correct statements from incorrect ones. Truth is not a category of existence. That which exists simply is, regardless of what words we use to describe it.

Myth and Ritual in the Origin of Language

There have been attempts to conscientiously shape language in a more objective direction, or form new languages *ex nihilo*, for a more Enlightened future population. Esperanto in particular comes to mind.

But all of these attempts have failed, and will continue to fail because the subjectivity inherent in language is precisely what makes it functional. Esperanto and other constructed language proselytizers seek unity through more neutral languages, but only wind up with monstrosities that lose depth and precision, and are usually accidentally biased toward one language group or another anyhow. Meanwhile conventional, organic languages maintain a versatility and flexibility that matches the breadth of subjective human experience.

Interestingly, conventional languages like English *do* possess a kind of stability. We can open a Shakespeare play and understand the clear meaning of the characters, despite 500 years of linguistic adaptation and evolution. Had English not experienced a profound injection of Danish and Norman French, we would likely still be able to read and understand a work like *Beowulf* without a translation. The internal evolution of a language can be broad, but is often not so deep as to render older works incomprehensible.

If languages truly are arbitrary and subjective, where does this firmness come from?

Anthropologist Roy Rappaport argued that the remarkable firmness of language – in spite of its own adaptive flexibility – can be understood to be a byproduct of religious ritual:

> ...certain defining elements of religion, especially the concept of the sacred and the process of sanctification, are no less possibilities of language, particularly of linguistic expression in ritual, than are lies, and that religion emerged with language. As such, religion is as old as language, which is to say precisely as old as humanity.[32]

Rappaport argued that the rigid invariance of performative ritual – actions which could have preceded "religion" proper – provided a point of reference and a kind of model for the invariant stability of grammar. Ritual establishes the sacred, the unchanging and unquestionable. And this unquestionable sanctity, in the established sacred, forms a bedrock upon which language can stand. Only with a solid foundation can it bend and flex as necessary for functional, everyday usage.

If, for example, you heard someone say "I gamboozled the most delicious goose yesterday," the invariant structure of the sentence – combined with the known semantic meaning of words like "delicious" and "goose" – provide a fairly reasonable guess as to the meaning of a nonsense word like "gamboozled." Structural rules and stability create greater possibilities for complexity and flexibility in meaning.

We can see more historical evidence of this invariant, sacral foundation for language in the significance of the *Iliad* for Greek and of the *King James Bible* for English. Both works were idiomatic constructs even for their day, highly formalized hybrids of dialect that were

---

32   Rappaport, Roy. *Ritual and Religion in the Making of Humanity.* 1999.

stylistically elevated above common speech, conveying the feeling of the sacred not only in semantic content, but in the language itself. Because of these features, these texts served as invariant foundations for meaning in their respective languages, despite not themselves modeling common language.

It is significant that these books did not merely exist, but were *recited* in a ritualistic fashion – by rhapsodes at the Panathenaic Games, and by priests at the mass, respectively. Performative repetition (especially in a sacred context) creates a linguistic anchor for a society – common reference points, understandings, associations, even pronunciations. These ritual-linguistic anchors create the firmness of form that give conventional languages their mutual comprehensibility, despite their organic movement and growth.

Now let us return to the Age of Reason, because it is through the examination of language that the tragedy of the Enlightenment comes into clearer focus: The fear of the blood feud led to a delegation of authority upward; the judgment of the higher arbiter required objectivity, and objectivity required the breaking of illusions and myths which might have justified or sanctioned individual retribution.

With the toppling of myths came the abandonment of rituals that were associated with myth, and ultimately, the setting of the sun into a postmodern condition, a cold night of meaninglessness. We feel this void in both our art and our language, and our experience reveals the connection between these two things. If reason requires language, and if language works by subjective comparison, then the flight from myth, the distrust in ritual, in art, and in all things *subjective* could not help but eventually erode reason itself, until we left ourselves in a Godless vacuum of our own creation.

This deicide was certainly not intended by the Greeks of the classical age or the Europeans of the 17th and 18th century. The wise men of the past were – by all appearances – simply seeking to mitigate the worst evil of their own days: the blood feud. Indeed, they succeeded in concluding the blood feud. They just could not have imagined the cost: movement toward a collapse of language itself as the subjective foundations of human experience are rejected in favor of increasingly sterile and cold notions of objectivity.

It is probably impossible for a full collapse to happen. Subjective beings like us are likely not capable of such a thing, even if we wanted that. But we experience the movement in that direction as a growing feeling of disconnection, distrust, and isolation – from others and from ourselves.

The question for us is: what do we do now?

PART 3

Phenomenology

We find the trailhead to a path out of the postmodern condition in a late 19th century philosopher named Edmund Husserl.

Husserl was a mathematician who recognized the trouble that Western philosophy was in, even before the beginning of WWII. He began his philosophical writing with an exploration of the psychological foundation for mathematics[33], but this gradually expanded into a broader philosophical project. Husserl sought to provide a new foundation for the edifice of Western philosophy, not on reason with Descartes, but on subjective experience itself. Husserl called his systematic, objective approach to studying subjective experience "phenomenology," deriving its name from the study of appearances. He believed that the path to real knowledge had to begin not by evading our subjective experience, but by facing it directly and systematically.

Husserl's approach was, in many ways, itself a symptom of Enlightenment thinking. But his concern was that contextualization in the domains of history, psychology (colloquially called "historicism" and "psychologism"), and even science would erode the possibility of knowledge – perhaps anticipating Thomas Kuhn's postmodern deconstruction of the psychology of science[34] by several decades[35]. He saw the way in which Reason created tools of analysis that undermined the possibility of Reason. It was Husserl's hope that through a systematic study of our own experience of the world, we might develop a science of experience which could then form a foundation for knowledge and save philosophy[36].

---

33   Husserl, Edmund, *The Philosophy of Arithmetic.* 1891.
34   Kuhn, Thomas, *The Structure of Scientific Revolutions.* 1962.
35   "...no objective science can do justice to the subjectivity that achieves science." Husserl, Edmund, "Philosophy and the Crisis of European Man." 1935.
36   Husserl's massive body of work is complex and changes slightly over the course of his life, and is somewhat hard to pin down simply. However, the transformation of philosophy into a kind of science was at least one of his goals.

While Husserl's yearning for a foundation for certainty put him in line with Enlightenment thinkers like Descartes and Kant, his pursuit took him in the opposite direction – not away from the senses, but *toward* the senses. This shift in direction required not merely going back to Descartes, but going all the way back to Plato, whose theory of the *Forms* set all of Western philosophy on a path of introspective reflection, of turning inward, into the mind.

Husserl's desire goes beyond reason, seeking to preserve the subjective culture that was built on the back of philosophy. But his shift back from the world of pure reason to the world of the senses was still driven by aspirations from the Age of Reason. Even his understanding of this philosophy – corresponding as it does with our genealogy of Reason, Justice, Objectivity, and Truth – does not escape the enchantment of Aeschylus, sifted through several layers of abstraction and historical interpretation:

> *Spiritually Europe has a birthplace. By this I do not mean a geographical place, in some one land, though this too is true. I refer, rather, to a spiritual birthplace in a nation or in certain men or groups of men belonging to this nation. It is the ancient Greek nation in the seventh and sixth centuries B.C. In it there grows up a new kind of attitude of individuals toward their environing world. Consequent upon this emerges a completely new type of spiritual structure, rapidly growing into a systematically rounded cultural form that the Greeks called philosophy. Correctly translated, in its original sense, this bespeaks nothing but universal science, science of the world as a whole, of the universal unity of all being.*[37]

The problem, of course, is that the whole enterprise begins not with the *belief* in the unity of all things, but with the *desire* that all things be unified. This desire is not objective and factual, but aesthetic in nature. Following from what we have learned about Aeschylus and the blood feud, a grand unity of existence – true objectivity – would negate the need for conflict, or find a common ground for resolving conflict. Without such unity, we might be faced with the declaration

---

37   Ibid.

of Achilles, that there can be no pacts between lions and men, that wolves and lambs can never be of one mind, but hate each other completely and forever. And of course, there is no truly objective reason why conflict should be avoided. Hume's Guillotine[38] remains as sharp as ever.

Husserl seemed to have an inkling of this. He believed in a "rational sense of life," which embraced almost romantic affirmations of culture, and that a "naïve objectivism" threatened this sense of life with a "barbarian hatred of spirit." Though his method failed to preserve this rational sense of life, his shift from the objective *noumenon* to the subjective *phenomenon* at least brought those good things in society back into focus, perhaps as something worth preserving.

Husserl's student Martin Heidegger picked up Husserl's phenomenology and took it in a less scientific direction. Heidegger sought to study Being, in the broadest sense, but believed we lacked the proper language and understanding to even begin such a study. He argued that we had to begin the investigation of "Being" through the study of "beings" – to study small things, not as a means of understanding the greater whole like naive reductionists, but to establish a foundation of experience in the world so that one day, we might hope to begin to study Being as a whole. This was to be done through *dasein* – literally, "being there" – by experiencing the world, and experiencing ourselves as perceiving agents in the world.

Some have claimed that Heidegger was an early existentialist – a movement popularized by Jean-Paul Sartre which begins with the belief that *existence precedes essence*. This view is an inversion of Neo-Platonism, which argues that essence precedes existence and that "forms" give rise to material things. But Heidegger rejected this label on linguistic grounds – he says these dichotomies and chicken-and-egg problems are meaningless without a proper language to discuss such things. There may or may not even be a distinction between an objects' "existence" and its "essence." What is essential

---

38   David Hume famously argued that no ethical imperatives follow from statements of fact – one cannot derive an "ought" from an "is."

is to begin with experiencing the world.

Heidegger's phenomenology also appears incomplete. Heidegger himself is unable to properly define "being," for precisely the reasons of language he gave in rejecting the label "existentialist." Being seems to be something we all know innately, and are at the same time profoundly ignorant of.

But in either case, his development of phenomenology from the pursuit of a science to the pursuit of presence takes us one step closer to a meaning in an age beyond the Age of Reason.

Perception and Experience as a Foundation for a New Phenomenology

Husserl focused on the method of studying our experience of the world, and Heidegger tried to focus more on the meaning of that experience. But what if phenomenology was taken more completely to its original Greek roots, and was understood directly as a study of appearances? Not as the study of *our experiences* of appearances, which in fact distracts us from the appearances themselves and draws us back into recursive introspection; nor as a study of the meaning of these experiences, which risks a collapse back into *a priori* linguistic categories and the siren song of objectivity and truth – what of a "phenomenology" that is simply observing and contemplating the world?

It is necessary to briefly explicate certain aspects of the experience of perception itself before a longer, philosophical exploration of perceptions can be undertaken. But this need not be a lengthy, methodological study. For our purposes, we need only remember that non-linguistic animals can also use their eyes, and see without seeing categories in linguistic form: a small predator instead of a "cat," a place to sit instead of a "chair," a red fruit instead of an "apple," and so forth. Their perception is unmediated by language.

Yet perception is limited by resolution – for other animals as well as for humans. When we see at a distance, we might make out only an outline, devoid of detail – we see a pattern, a kind of "form," but not of the Platonic kind inferred from idealized purpose. This is especially noticeable at lower light, or at rapid speeds, as when we glimpse an image only for a fraction of a second.

These patterns strike us not as categorical identities, but as cues for *valences* – often triggering our emotions and reactions even before our "higher" brains have worked out how to describe and consciously understand what it is we are looking at. We perceive first a cue for fear, or a cue for hunger, or a cue for disgust, awe, or sexual desire. A non-language-speaking animal sees and responds to what it sees in such a fashion. It does not have the cognitive ability – nor perhaps the need – to linguistically "identify" and categorize what it sees, only to respond to it correctly. And humans developed our sense of sight with these lower animals, long before we developed our capacity for complex language.

Naming things is like ascribing number to physical objects. It can be incredibly useful, but names are not "true" in any objective sense. So, in the pursuit of the *phenomenon*, what if objectivity is abandoned as an aim?

We have established that Aeschylus was the mythical source of the eventual transition into the linguistic ideal of "truth." This transformation happened because truth is *objective*, and was in turn believed to *be* objective because of the good intentions revealed in those who seek the disinterested (objective) truth. The value of objectivity was the salvation it offered from vengeance – a binding, higher authority by which the spirit of revenge could be restrained and transformed. "True justice" – as opposed to the vengeance of the Furies – is itself revealed to be what is objective, what is true, and what is driven by good intentions.

A crude formula for the spirit of the Enlightenment could be written as follows: *justice = good intentions = objectivity = truth*.

But we have seen the magic and the illusion behind this formula, well-intentioned though it was. An emphasis on the importance of truth cannot itself survive if the mythic foundation for its value is, itself, *not true*. Justice is not the same as truth, nor is truth identical with objectivity, nor is objectivity the same as justice. The linguistic spell is broken, and has been broken, ever since the 20th century revealed the separation between good intentions and peace. As philosopher Daniel Dennett has often repeated, the 20th century taught us nothing if not the fact that the road to Hell is paved with good intentions.

But when we go back to the roots, we can find hints of an alternative ideal in the very language of justice. Indeed, there is an inflection point in the language of what is idealized in speech, at the transition point from pre-modern thought to "modernist" thinking. We see this inflection point most clearly in the language of Socrates in his trial, where he says:

> I shall use the words and arguments which occur to me at the moment; for I am certain that this is right [dikaia].[39]

Shortly thereafter, Socrates contrasts himself with his accusers, who speak in an ornamented[40] manner. Socrates says that he will speak àtechnōs – literally, "without skill." He claims that if he is persuasive, it is because he speaks the truth [aletheia]. This is a seedling hint of Enlightenment ideas, yet his proclaimed mode of speech champions the pre-Enlightenment ideal of plain and direct speech. As mentioned previously, Socrates compared himself to Achilles, and in the *Iliad*, we see Achilles address the embassy from Agamemnon in the following manner:

> I will say it outright [dokeî]. That seems best [àrista] to me.[41]

---

39   Plato, Apology. 17c.

40   The Greek word is κεκοσμημένους, which stems from the root *kosmeo*, and implies ordering and arranging things in a planned and skillful fashion.

41   Homer, *Iliad*. 9.315.

Shining through in the language of Socrates is the pre-Aeschelian ideal of directness, not because it is *true* in a manner that is binding because it is objective, but because it is *best*. Socrates speaks directly because it seems "just." But "just" had acquired its feeling of righteousness because to that point, direct and clear speech was best. It had inherited a positive valence from an older world.

As a matter of perception, "truth" is unknowable. But "best" is a valence we see or feel directly, sometimes even before we can identify the object of our attention. Unlike truth, goodness (or its absence) is often recognizable directly through our subjective senses.

The pre-Enlightenment ideal of speech was not "truth" but "clarity" ("clarity" being the source of the experience of excellence in speech). This clarity was described as *dike*, and corresponded with a broader pre-Enlightenment ideal of "good" (*ariston*) over the Enlightenment preference for "objectivity." What is best is at odds with what is objective, since objectivity is neutrality, while "best" expresses a subjective preference.

Likewise, if "truth" is something that must be uncovered – and if there is always something beneath the thing unearthed – then clarity in speech is at odds with the valence of truth. Truth must tend toward increasing complexity, toward caveats and layers of nuance and contextualization, as we often see in scientific or technical writing. But clarity speaks directly, *dike*, without need to affirm itself *as true*.

Some philosophers will say that this notion of "clarity," as an ideal in opposition to "truth" is in fact a theory of truth – namely, the *correspondence* theory of truth, as opposed to the *coherence* theory of truth. But again, if we look to the original usages of "truth," by those who claimed to speak "the truth," they were always speaking in opposition to the senses. The very idea of "Truth" opposes the naive correspondence held by the masses. And the word "truth" is, in any case, not necessary to describe what appears before us. It is sufficient to say "we see this." Against the simplicity and clarity of perception, claims to possession of the "truth" commit the sin of supererogation.

Here, we must address perhaps the oldest critique of the philosophers: that we cannot trust our senses. It is said that the senses can be deceived.

If we look more closely, we notice that it is not the senses which are unreliable, but our *interpretation of the senses* – here we are on firm Kantian ground. Our interpretation of our sense data is drawn largely from experience and pattern recognition. When our "senses" are deceived, it is because the background experience and knowledge we possess, and through which we perceive the world, is incomplete. This is how magic tricks and illusions usually work: they use our natural experience and pattern recognition skills to trick our mind into inferring something, "filling in the gaps" in our perceptual blindspots with something intuitive but which did not actually happen. We may feel as if we "saw it with our own eyes," when in fact we did not.

Once we experience these kinds of deceptions, a natural skepticism comes to inoculate us from the dangers of directly identifying what we think we see with "the truth." When watching a magic show, or a news report, we might replace the mental thought "this happened" with "this appeared to have happened.

Here, deductive notions of "truth" are not an answer to illusions, but often the source of them. A highly educated person who "sees no other explanation" is far more likely to feel forced to accept a false or deceptive conclusion, as if the world were comprised of logical syllogisms. It is often the layman who is content to judge that something "seems off," and retreat from dubious and manipulative assertions into agnostic skepticism – not the all-rejecting skepticism of postmodernism, but the discrete skepticism of trusting one's own body and senses.

So long as we remember this point, the critique of the reliability of the senses (in correctly deducing truth about the external world) is not a critique of the senses at all, but is in fact a critique of our experience and pattern recognition. If the problem is insufficient experience, then the critique of the reliability of the senses boils down to a complaint about incomplete knowledge. It is a tragic irony that this inadequacy of experience is then used to justify criticizing trust in the very mechanism by which we acquire more experience: the senses.

When we frame things correctly and recognize the role that experience plays in both perception and in the "deception of the senses," the critique of the senses becomes circular: the fact that we don't already know everything – in fact, *cannot* know everything – is used to argue that we should not trust our senses at all, and should look for "knowledge" elsewhere... perhaps into our mind, as though our faculties of analysis and logic were somehow less prone to fault.
This is the justification for philosophical systems, grand theories of epistemology and the vain pursuit of *a priori* knowledge, grounded in coherence models of "truth." But if the same, excavating instinct for truth is directed at these systems, they are all found wanting – no less than the senses (or, again, our powers of interpretation from sense data).

All of these systems and theories depend upon logical axioms which are themselves not logically justified – in fact *cannot* be logically justified, and which may be accurate but incomplete in their description of the world. Newtonian physics is accurate but incomplete, as an explanation of movement. Evolution by natural selection is accurate but incomplete, as an explanation of speciation and biological change.

Both Newtonian physics and Darwinian evolution only remain useful when they are understood and applied in the manner that they were discovered – through sense observation. The moment they become doctrinal axioms, the events that occur beyond the scope of their presuppositions become contradictions, and a useful theory becomes "false." This applies to all Grand Theories.

The more intuitive and practical answer to deception, ignorance, and inexperience is simply this: more experience.

Perhaps it is time for a new phenomenology that emphasizes experience itself, over the study *of* experience.

Myth, Language, and Solar Phenomenology

There may be a temptation to assume that if we are to reject the Age of Reason in pursuit of this new phenomenology, we must therefore go back and 'pick up where we left off.' Should we then "believe in" the myths and the Gods that were rejected in the name of reason?

If we assume that the pre-Enlightenment ideal was "clarity" and not "truth," as it aligns with our perceptual experience of the world, and if our perceptions begin as valence-experiences, then it becomes clear that asking "are the gods 'true'?" was always the wrong question. It is an Enlightenment question not suitable for subjective eyes.

We see the heroes of the pre-Enlightenment age described as "shining" [*dîos*[42]] like the sun, or "like a god" [*daimōn īsos*[43]]. The implication is that the Gods do not exist in the domain of "truth," which is not what we perceive anyhow, but rather exist in the domain of *valence*. They appear as expressions of personified purity of form, which we perceive and share with each other. The grand and terrible powers of the earth have a common experience. The theory of plate tectonics is undoubtedly useful and predictive, but whether or not it is "true" has little bearing on how we experience an earthquake. The power has a certain character to it, and the ancients gave a name to the pure form of this valence: Poseidon. If we look not to "true"

---

42   Ibid. 1.7. Note: *dîos* is sometimes translated as "godlike."
43   Ibid. 16.705. Note: Greg Nagy translates *daimōn* not as "god" but as "superhuman force"; for our purposes here, the transcendent nature of the description is the same.

comparisons in mechanics but instead to similarities in experience, we immediately understand why the thundering gallop of hooves might cause the ancients to also associate horses with Poseidon, or connect the great eagle, striking suddenly from the sky, with the lightning of heavenly Zeus.

In a valence-centered view of human perception, we find a foundation for religious experience, one which is likely similar to that religious experience of the world which existed before the Myth of Enlightenment set in motion the death of the gods.

But this is not a call to "return." Perhaps some of the ancients *did* believe the gods were "true." If so, perhaps the elevation of truth – and the development of scientific methods for exploring nature – has demonstrated that they were wrong. An idea is not more true because it existed in the past. We have seen the shortcomings of elevating "truth." Without "truth" as an ideal, we are left to begin with perception, and with all the subjective experiences that come with it, regardless of what those in the past believed, in all of their wide-ranging variety.

But perception is not the conclusion; it is only a beginning.

The postmodernists were simultaneously right and wrong: they recognized the failure of the Enlightenment, but were themselves so caught up in the ideal of "truth" and "objectivity" that they could never let go of the mission, and fell either into a compulsion toward objective nihilism, or into twisting these rationalist ideals into increasingly convoluted and totalitarian systems that they hoped might finally bring about the elusive utopia.

We have described how this new phenomenology replaces the ideal of "truth" with that of "clarity, and replaces the pursuit of "objectivity" with the pursuit of what is "best." But there is a third pre-Enlightenment ideal: we must also replace "systems" with "judgment." Judgment, as we have described, was closely related with clarity and goodness. It was how decisions were made without some algorithm or system to make decisions for us. And as we have seen, the subjective assumptions at the root of all systems means that there can be no truly objective system anyhow; their axioms require subjective judgment. The necessity of judgment is inescapable.

Systems can certainly aid us in our aims, but they cannot take away our responsibility in choosing those aims. They cannot replace our mind any more than they can replace our eyes. And judgment is a skill, a virtue that we develop by means of experience. To systematize our experiences in a scientific manner – to "control the variables" – would in fact be to limit our experiences and to limit our capacity to judge, making us more naive, less virtuous, more prone to the manipulations of magic and illusion that take advantage of a limited range of experience.

Judgment requires ideals. To say "this is better than that" is an inescapably subjective claim, and also a claim that is relative to different kinds of experience – to different *valences of perception*.

The Gods may be pure forms of these valences, but they are not necessarily beings to be emulated *per se*. They are forces to be respected and accounted for, but they remain beyond our reach.

This here is perhaps the answer to the *hliðskjálf dilemma*: we may hold Odin's throne in our hand, but for all the vision, for all the opportunity for power, we lack his flaming eye. *We are not God.*

Our limited experience constrains our powers of perception and understanding, even through technologically magnified eyes. Our new phenomenology reminds us of our limitations, and cures us of the belief in objectivity. Indeed, recognizing the limitations of our perception reminds us that *the dilemma is itself an illusion.*

For all the information we have about the world and its myths, we *know* much less than we believe we know. Information is not knowledge because mere information is devoid of the context and valence that allows us to make meaningful and accurate use of information.

And this understanding is not itself "more information." It is an understanding of the relationships between things, an understanding which precedes language, and therefore can never be fully conveyed through language. We can be primed to appreciate and grasp this knowledge through language, but we can only begin to truly possess this knowledge through experience.

This understanding does not stop us from taking a wide look, across countries and across time, for aspirational ideals. To descend Odin's throne is to descend *into* this exploration. A broad, even syncretic view of the world becomes a source of experience that improves judgment and perception and clarity in thought. By exploration, we come to develop taste, and begin to understand new ideals.

The ideals we strive for – what is best – are embodied in heroes who shine like the immortals. We see them as *larger than life*, because their excellence strikes us at the level of perception. They become models, and center points – along with the Gods – in rituals that create language and create our sense of self through this creation of language. On the high peak, holding the objective view of the world, is the Sun alone. The sun becomes the unreachable, yet nonetheless aspirational, ideal that illuminates the task of experience and the development of other ideals.

"Solar phenomenology" then picks up where Husserl and Heidegger left off, and applies it in our relationship to the world. Solar phenomenology is the study of how things appear to us, directly, with a full embrace of the idiosyncratic diversity of appearances. It does not make claims to universal, objective truth, because this cannot be known to us – it belongs to the sun alone.

As a study of what is seen under the sun, Solar Phenomenology pursues the divine surface, with a seasoned understanding of the limitations of our own experience in correctly perceiving the world. It rejects and even mocks "grand systems" designed to stand in the place of human vision and judgment, while at the same time adopting an empiricist's interest in systems for exploration and discovery. It rejects the neutrality and impossibility of "objectivity" with the positive embrace of "good," and with it, the task of refining our taste of the good by experience.

Solar phenomenology embraces significance of myth, and the inextricable relationship between ritual and language, just as it acknowledges light as the source of vision, and so begins its ritual embrace of myth with an embrace of the sun itself. In the light of the sun, the Gods shine through as emanations not of truth, but of clarity, and heroes burn like stars in the constellations of our own lives.

The Importance of the Body

Solar phenomenology is not the phenomenology of Husserl or Heidegger, which attempted to direct its gaze inward into the process of perception; there the phenomenon was a means by which we were to study ourselves. Solar phenomenology is satisfied with the phenomena itself – understanding that there is some relationship between ourselves and the world, but unconcerned with working out the precise details of that relationship in theoretical terms, prior to experience.

However, solar phenomenology is still a study. It is not a collapse into relativism, accepting our varying and sometimes competing experiences of the world as *equal*, not least because on their face they do not appear as equal. A superficial (which is here sufficient) study of appearances reveal broad patterns of agreement in what constitutes beauty and goodness. Health is better than sickness. Strength is better than weakness. Intelligence is better than stupidity. We value symmetry, balance, grace, and other signs of life and health. And within any number of more precise domains, patterns of preference emerge among those with the most experience.

It is readily apparent that our personal condition modifies our taste and aesthetic appreciation. From Nietzsche asserting that we necessarily have "the philosophy of one's personality"[44] to Mishima's

---

44   Nietzsche, Friedrich. *The Joyful Wisdom*. 1882.

meditations on the "nocturnal thought" of the men with "dry, lus-terless skins and sagging stomachs"[45], we – humans – have observed the relationship between the body and thought since the days of Aristotle, who noticed that people more highly value health when they are ill, wealth when they are poor, and so forth[46].

As a pursuit of excellence, clarity, and good judgment, Solar phe-nomenology does not merely study appearances, but approaches appearances as they appear to healthy, strong, life-affirming eyes – to the tastes of the *form* of being that we ourselves wish to emulate. Thus, the *body* becomes a key to unlocking our approach to clarity, excellence, and judgment. This is not to say that solar phenome-nology requires innate physical excellence, nor even that all with strong and healthy bodies will possess this frame of mind. Mishima and Nietzsche were themselves both *decadents*[47] who turned their natural skills and tendencies away from the pursuit of truth through language (both having gone further in that direction than most of humanity could ever hope to travel), and instead redirected efforts toward appearance and health.

If solar phenomenology owes a debt in groundwork to Husserl, Heidegger, and Gadamer, it owes just as much of a debt to the self-overcoming work of Nietzsche and Mishima, who managed to overpower their own nocturnal tendencies in the pursuit of clarity, excellence, and judgment. They did this by finding the roots of these virtues, which were not incorporal abstractions, but present in the world, right there in their own bodies. Both thinkers used the body as a tool to explore thought, by long hikes in the mountains and by rigorous outdoor physical training, respectively.

A phenomenology that neglects the body cannot be relied upon in the pursuit of excellence because our body is the very thing that per-ceives the world. The unhealthy and the ugly will tend to subvert and reverse all appearances for the sake of power, as we see occurring

---

45   Mishima, Yukio. *Sun and Steel*. 1968.
46   Aristotle. *Nicomachean Ethics* 1.4.
47   Nietzsche describes a "decadent" as someone with a spiritual condition which renders them excessively sensitive, especially to pain.

in various political movements today.

However, there are also those who pursue "truth" by delving far into a single category. They dedicate themselves completely to a single field. Such people cannot help but grow to interpret the world through this field – the engineer sees the problems of the world as engineering problems; the business manager perceives managing problems; the physical trainer perceives physical problems, and so forth. An implicit solipsism creeps into thought through excessive specialization. They come to believe they can understand many things through one thing, and this error often expresses itself in their very bodies, showing a disproportionality or neglect that mirrors the eccentric, unbalanced focus of their thinking, which follows from axiomatic thought. The body is essential for the pursuit of solar phenomenology, but it too can become a solipsistic specialization that inhibits the development of greater experience.

We can see an example of this solar ideal embodied in the Roman lawyer and philosopher, Cicero, and in the American statesman, George Washington.

In *De Oratore*, Cicero attempts to address the question: 'why are there so few good speakers?' Given the ubiquity of speech, one would expect there to be more great speakers than there are great generals, great artisans, and so forth, but in his estimation, truly great rhetoricians are fewer than masters of any other field. Sophists believe that one can simply learn persuasive speech, and in doing so, exert their influence over others in all subjects and in all conversations (and make their money on the promise that their teachings will have exactly this effect). But Cicero disagrees, saying that to actually speak well requires knowledge and experience about all things one might speak about, and the rarity of truly excellent speakers is not due to a shortage of sophists to teach them, but the enormity of experience required of the individual to truly begin to know what he is talking about:

In my opinion, indeed, no man can be an orator possessed of every praiseworthy accomplishment, unless he has attained the knowledge of everything important, and of all liberal arts, for his language must be ornate and copious from knowledge, since, unless there be beneath the surface matter understood and felt by the speaker, oratory becomes an empty and almost puerile flow of words [...] But because this, I doubt not, will appear to most people an immense and infinite undertaking...[48]

Cicero is widely remembered as a lawyer and politician, where his skill saved the Roman Republic from the Second Catilinarian Conspiracy. But he was so successful as a speaker – a skill required in law and politics – because he was also a soldier, an academic translator, and a student of architecture. His skill as a speaker reflected a wide-ranging knowledge from experience, rather than a purely legalistic exhortation from axiomatic first principles.

In a similar manner, George Washington was best known for being the first president of the United States, at least after the ratification of the 1789 Constitution. But beyond being a mere politician, Washington was a surveyor, a farmer, an inventor, a soldier, a general, and a spy-master. He was even described by Thomas Jefferson as "the best horseman of his age." Washington's success as a leader, and the ultimate success of America, were largely the results of a wide-ranging interest in virtually all things under the sun.

Both Cicero and Washington traveled extensively, if not necessarily widely. Their bodies as well as their thought reflected a breadth of experience. Contrasted with the isolated, priest-like bodies and the scholastic, deductive logic that marked Enlightenment philosophers like Descartes and Kant[49], Washington and Cicero were described as tall and graceful men, with strong, athletic bodies and handsome faces.

---

48   Cicero. *De Oratore.*
49   Rene Descartes stood at 5'1"; Immanuel Kant was 5'2".

Solar Phenomenology for Tomorrow

The illusions of the Age of Reason are dying – not yet dead, but mortally wounded. It was not killed by the postmodernists; they only saw the signs first. Yet the postmodernists themselves are the contorted products of Enlightenment thought, desperately fighting to resuscitate its ideals of objectivity and truth. Indeed, the compulsion to *be* jaded and disillusioned is a shadowy remnant of the obligation to be objective. It carries forward the Enlightenment dissatisfaction with appearances and the rejection of myth, simply adding its own suspicion and dissatisfaction with Enlightenment systems. One could say that postmodernism is simply Enlightenment thinking applied consistently, and turned upon itself.

If we go about purging all myth, only to find that the very motivation to rid ourselves of myth was *itself* mythical, we are no longer obligated to carry that iconoclastic instinct past the destruction of the Enlightenment *anti-myth*. We can let go of this destructive compulsion, along with the Age of Reason, because we can see that objective reason will eventually destroy everything including itself.

We can appreciate the Age of Reason as a part of our history, as the well-meaning attempt of the ancients to constrain the worst evil of their time – the blood feud. We can even commend its success in accomplishing this goal. Its champions could not have known the price in advance – not just in terms of warfare on an unprecedented scale, but in the decline of personal virtues and excellence, of honor, and the heralding of the Last Man – in the destruction of our culture and of our society.

Solar Phenomenology is a philosophical path to meaning and direction. It is a road out of the void that we created by believing that purpose must be tethered to Truth, without realizing that objective Truth negates subjective purposes. This path begins with the embrace of the subjective, not merely as an end in itself, but as the necessary and only vehicle by which we can experience what exists *outside* of our bodies.

Solar Phenomenology will not solve global warfare. Nor will it end the modern state, or any such thing. Its aim is not negation of that kind, even the negation of things we think of as harmful. Instead it pursues what is desirable, what is good. Since disinterested objectivity does not end violence (even if it does end the smaller-scale violence of the blood feud), we are free to return to what is *best*. Truth, an ideal which emerged from objectivity, did not perform its justifying function – indeed, we never successfully disentangled the statements we wished to describe *as* true from the word "truth." We are therefore free to once again prefer *clarity*. Since our systems failed to achieve true objectivity, we are free once again to develop *judgment*.

Culture – the material and social substance of living human societies – cannot survive the scrutiny of objectivity, truth, and systematization. In condemning myth and rejecting the subjective, we see that what was truly being condemned by the Enlightenment was *us*, at the very level of our power of perception. The Age of Reason told us that humans live in darkness, in ignorance. To become "enlightened" by reason is, at some level, to transcend our own humanity; and the drive for Enlightenment is the drive to negate Humanity. Fortunately, these aims cannot be achieved completely, even in theory, because they are the products of subjective human beings. As aspirational ideals, they remain subjective. But this leaves everything open to criticism from a higher, more destructive position of objectivity, because of the idealization of objectivity and reason. The Age of Reason invites postmodernism and the devouring of all culture.

But the pursuit of clarity, goodness, and judgment cannot help but create culture because it affirms our own being. It does this by affirming our vision. And faith in our own power of perception is also praise to the Sun, which makes vision both possible and good, and not an illusion to be distrusted and escaped.

This reorientation does not reject the *use of objectivity* as a means to pursue some end – for instance, a man employing a scientific process of objective investigation in order to build a bridge, or to become stronger, or to strengthen his marriage. The desire for the bridge, for muscles, or for a relationship was not itself a scientific premise, but a personal desire for what is good, unbound by any need to justify itself to "truth." Relative objectivity in method is justified by the good, rather than goodness judged against some ever-receding standard of objectivity.

The pursuit of excellence, clarity, and judgment requires experience. We must begin – as Aristotle says – with doing things:

Now each man judges well the things he knows, and of these he is a good judge. And so the man who has been educated in a subject is a good judge of that subject, and the man who has received an all-round education is a good judge in general. Hence a young man is not a proper hearer of lectures on political science; for he is inexperienced in the actions that occur in life, but its discussions start from these and are about these[...][50]

In advancing Solar Phenomenology as an alternative to the Age of Reason, four questions arise:

First, do we need to go about actively bringing the Enlightenment to an end?

Second, what are we to do about the postmodernists?

Third, what should we do about blood feuds, if blood feuds are to re-emerge in the absence of the intellectual constructs that have held them at bay?

And fourth: is there still any place for philosophy in Solar Phenomenology?

The collapse of the Enlightenment and its ideals will generate a vacuum – exactly the "death of God" articulated by Nietzsche which we have already described. It is true that we have already begun

---

50   Aristotle, Nichomachean Ethics. 1.3.

to experience this void, but our society has not collapsed. The decaying body of the Enlightenment is temporarily filling the void, and perhaps this placeholder is desirable to have, however temporary it may be. It seems unlikely that good ideas are best achieved in the heat of chaos – or, if they are, they are achieved at a high human price by trial and error. There is very little cost in working under an existing Enlightenment-based system while we contemplate what might come next.

But further, it is not clear just how dependent our existing systems are upon Enlightenment values. The trial of Aeschylus speaks of "justice," but the trial of the blood price on Achilles' shield speaks of no such abstractions. It only describes the conflict, and offers a reward to whoever speaks best, in explicit terms of clarity and judgment [*dike*]. One could imagine many more-or-less modern social and political institutions that do good work, saved by a Herculean re-grounding onto stronger, Mythic foundations.

It appears unwise to accelerate the death of what is already dying. It is better to make productive use of that time to prepare for what comes afterward, rather than to rush into a void in the hopes of devising a plan once we arrive.

This brings us to the second question: what should we do about the postmodernists, who seem intent upon rushing us into this void?
Much of the critique of postmodernism comes from a liberal (Enlightenment) frame of mind. It counters the postmodern deconstruction of truth with a positive defense of truth, not recognizing that the postmodern position is in fact a more advanced stage of the Enlightenment project. By contrast, the Solar approach, and the counter to the destructive impulse of postmodernism, is creation. This new creation must be built upon a more defensible hill. But this is not difficult when the justification for new culture is not "objective truth" but "subjective good." There is no postmodern criticism of this.

A postmodernist might ask pointedly if something is "truly good" – thereby revealing a latent loyalty to, or cynical abuse of, objectivity. But such a challenge loses its corrosive power when objectivity was never the justification or aim. Creation done explicitly for the subjective good is beyond the jurisdiction of the postmodernist.

But after this creation, what will we do about blood feuds, should they return?

Let us set aside the obvious fact that war on a global scale is far worse than a blood feud, and that even if we simply had to live with blood feuds again, it would likely be an acceptable trade-off if we were able to rid ourselves of industrial modern war in the process[51]. Blood feuds were still the worst evils of their day, and are no small problem to simply accept.

We are here rejecting the complete answer to the blood feud – Aeschylus' transformation of "justice" and the subsequent Age of Reason – because the cure has been worse than the disease. But this does not mean we have to accept the disease untreated. Given the mythical stories we have already discussed, it is safe to say that falling back on myth gives us plenty of inspiration and advice against resentment and engaging in cycles of violence. Mythic example may not be enough to end blood feuds, but perhaps they can inspire circumspection and mitigate the worst of their fatal consequences. Finally, and somewhat paradoxically: is there any room for philosophy in Solar Phenomenology?

In the life of Socrates, we see philosophy depicted as a kind of medicine for the disease of ignorance which he believed caused such pain and suffering. But it is not clear that philosophy is, in fact, a cure to ignorance, let alone suffering. From Aristotle, we are told that philosophy without experience is dangerous and irresponsible, and indeed, with experience, philosophy itself may be superfluous. Philosophy

---

51   While grand wars did occasionally happen in pre-Enlightenment society, they did not tend to exist in *pre-civilized* society. The trade-off between civilization and large-scale warfare remains a problem, but perhaps less so for civilizations whose legitimacy does not hinge upon the negation of conflict.

does not seem to be necessary, nor even beneficial, personally or civically. Insofar as philosophy created the Enlightenment, philosophy may be closer to a disease than a cure. Is philosophy then to be abandoned?

I believe philosophy must necessarily be devalued, relative to its current place of honor... but it need not be abandoned. Just as philosophers existed prior to Socrates (and indeed, Nietzsche argues that these were perhaps the best philosophers), so can we philosophize in the absence of Socrates' confusion of philosophy with medicine. The pre-Socratics did not philosophize to save us from ignorance, but for its own sake. Even in Socrates, we can find a pre-Enlightenment justification for philosophy: as a form of worship of the Gods, and following divine signs like his own inner *dæmon*:

> Hitherto the familiar oracle within me has constantly been in the habit of opposing me even about trifles, if I was going to make a slip or error about anything; and now as you see there has come upon me that which may be thought, and is generally believed to be, the last and worst evil. But the oracle made no sign of opposition, either as I was leaving my house and going out in the morning, or when I was going up into this court, or while I was speaking, at anything which I was going to say; and yet I have often been stopped in the middle of a speech; but now in nothing I either said or did touching this matter has the oracle opposed me. What do I take to be the explanation of this? I will tell you. I regard this as a proof that what has happened to me is a good, and that those of us who think that death is an evil are in error. This is a great proof to me of what I am saying, for the customary sign would surely have opposed me had I been going to evil and not to good.[52]

We have seen science abused and corrupted, transformed from a method of pursuing knowledge of the world into a system for browbeating and dominating others in the domain of civic policy. This abuse in turn corrupted science itself, in its methodology and integrity, as the interest of power often finds greater use in fraud and misinterpretation than in curious and slow exploration. A similar

---

52   Plato. *Apology.*

dynamic exists in philosophy, and a similar solution too. Philosophy is not itself a problem, any more than science is a problem – the problem is the civic application of science or philosophy to grand problems of human existence that are perhaps ineradicable – problems like ignorance, hubris, and vengeance.

These are not problems that science or philosophy can solve because the single source of these problems is *us*. To solve such problems would require a grand system to replace human action and choice comprehensively.

Solar Phenomenology approaches these problems individually, and *in the individual*. It is not "individualism" (nor is it "collectivism"), but a recognition of the importance of language and the body in our experience of the world, and a rejection of any attempt to understand – let alone save – the world without an initial foundation in judgment based upon experience.

By affirming our own vision, we affirm ourselves and our power to address the problems in life without turning them into a problem *of* life. After all, we often find examples of beauty, nobility, and excellence alongside experiences of loss, sadness, and despair. The literary genre of tragedy exemplifies the bittersweet experience of these pairings. To the degree that tragedies capture some general quality of life, they present us with a choice: do we focus our gaze upon the suffering, as something intolerable that must be cured? Or do we instead focus our eyes on the good, made all the more excellent by its contrast with the inevitable pain that comes with life?

The sensitive, weak body may be compelled by survival instinct to focus upon the pain, in hopes of mitigating its own suffering. But with a strong body, and a strong, enduring psychology that comes with such a body, it becomes possible to redirect our gaze to the positive – toward the beautiful, the noble, aspirational, and ideal. These ideals are not an aversion of our gaze from the suffering latent in existence, but rather treat the excellent as a redemption of the pain. The good makes endurance worthwhile.

Metaphysically, life is not merely pain. But pain *is* an inescapable component of life – a feedback mechanism for injury and danger. Without pain, we die. The root of pain is in our very bodies, and there is no escape from pain except death. An excessive hatred of pain can blur seamlessly into a hatred of life.

It takes a strong body to affirm ourselves in spite of the pain, to embrace life in the face of death, to trust our own senses when our senses are so often the very source of suffering. But with a resilience that begins with the body, and with direct experience of the world, we can find purpose and meaning and a love for ourselves, and for the good in humanity – as humans – in all of our organic complexity and messiness. This purpose and love does not require abstractions or "pure" ideas, of the sort that offer priestly escapism from the suffering. Rather it comes from the personal virtues of endurance, motion, and curiosity, which we pursued in the first place because they appeared to us as excellent.

And in time, we may once again see a civilization that is good, that is rising like the sun, illuminated by the light of clarity, and which is ours because it is good in *our* judgment, in *our* eyes.

LYRICS + POETRY

INTO THE LIGHT
LYRICS AND COMMENTARY BY PAUL BEGADON

These bodies are trapped in a world of the flesh.
Aging and slinking down into death.
This is the realm of matter, not mind,
But there's another world, far high above
the fleshy existence.
A world where our eye is overwhelmed
by sensations our brains can't descry.
That world is pure, noble, bright
And it's real. You know it.
It lights up the night.
That world is golden, and every atom of air
shines in the dark with a million years
Worth of stories and wisdom,
guidance, and joy.
There stands a long line of men
Back to Troy, back to Hector and Priam
And man-slaying Cain.
A long line of men who lived out their tale
And rose into legend leaving only their name
As lights on the headland
To show us the way.

Sometimes in the night
we can sense that high realm,
piercing the sky,
raining drops out of heaven
Down through the air
And into our minds.

We can flee from these moments,
Hide in the night.
Or lift up our eyes to heavenly skies
With courage in heart, mouths open wide
To taste drops of gold that fall from a high
and ideal world that's beyond our reach.
We can reach for it anyway.
Stretch out and grasp at the heavens
Lest we sink in the mud.
Because stagnant existence is poison, no good.

Look around you.
You see it,
People suffer in pain.
They've rejected the cosmos,
forgotten their place.
They don't see the light
of that heaven on high.
can't taste the gold-drops
that fall from the sky.

So I look to the past
and this question I ask,
How should I live?
What's my goal?
What's my task?

What mode of being is better
than this?
What works and what doesn't?

What's better, what's best?

Then I try to live up to what's best if I can.
And if I can't I try anyway and failure be damned.
But before you can live some idealized life,
You must see and must love that heavenly light.

So follow the trail of gold from on high
that fall from heaven.
You'll find them in stories of old on dark nights,
And those stories will lead you
Into the light.

Editor's Note

"Into the Light" was performed by Paul Begadon in a moving track produced by fellow Order of Fire member Fredrik Hejdenberg under his band name, Temple Tribe, in 2023.

"Into the Light" is currently available on all popular streaming sources, and a lyric video can be found on The Order of Fire's YouTube channel.

Commentary by Paul Begadon

The purpose of everything I write is to help us live better lives by exploring and applying the wisdom that has been handed down to us through the ages. I need wisdom as much as you probably do. I write, perhaps paradoxically, because I need answers, not because I have them. I find answers to many of my questions in the old stories that we've inherited from the generations who came before.

Those predecessors, those men only dimly visible through the mists of antiquity, lived their lives in much the same way that we do. They were born into a world that was indifferent and often hostile to their existence. They struggled to find a purpose in life, to find a worthy goal to move towards. They struggled to make progress toward that ideal, and along the way, before they died, they faced and resolved a lot of problems.

We're no different.

Sure, we have more advanced technology and different social and cultural norms to affect us. But men are men, and they live remarkably similar lives no matter where, or when, they come from.

The great thing about people is that we're storytellers. Some are better than others, but people can't stop telling stories. Which is good news, because it means we invent, develop, and pass on stories about the problems we've encountered and the solutions we've devised to overcome those problems. As those stories move through time, they get dramatized and updated to be more culturally relevant.

But the core of a story, its warm and beating heart, is some fragile shard of wisdom that our ancestors want us to know so that we're not crushed by problems that have already been resolved.

I'm not an academic or an expert in language or literature. I'm just a man who hasn't had a lot of guidance in life. For the most part, I've had to figure things out for myself or seek out people who can teach me what I need to know. I realized long ago that the collective human experience has been codified and handed down from one generation to the next in the stories we tell. If stories survive a long time, it's because they have something timeless to pass on. That led me to study old myths and legends, and there I found a treasure hoard of wisdom that I could apply to my own life.

The wisdom contained in the so-called "Classics" is sometimes specific and plainly stated, sometimes shrouded and veiled in narrative and poetry, but almost always it appears to relate to a specific culture in a particular time.

But that same localized and culturally singular wisdom is also universal. Just because we today are a millennia or more removed from the words and thoughts of some poet, some storyteller, some man, who composed an epic piece of literature that echoes through the ages, doesn't mean that we can't understand the meaning of his words and benefit from his experience.

I think you'll find that some things never change, not even after many centuries of human cultural progress. The advice written down by our far-distant predecessors may sound archaic, but its meaning is as relevant now as it's ever been. Perhaps more relevant now because it seems to have been forgotten. So we can continue to live well today by living the way people of the past lived well. This means that what was true in the past is still true today, which implies that there's some universal mode of being that works successfully across time.

The way we live might change, but the way to live well is the same now as it's ever been. That's encouraging if you ask me.

So dive into the old stories. Don't just read them. I'm not writing this to convince you to just "read the classics."

I mean dive into them. Put yourself into the old stories and explore what they have to tell you. Assume each story does, in fact, have something to tell you. Something important, with the potential to improve your life.

It might sound like hippy-dippy nonsense, but it's not. People who lived and died long ago are literally speaking to you, to YOU, and telling you about the things they thought, saw, suffered, and conquered. But they're dead and their voices have been stilled, so now they must speak in story.

That's enough words from me, so let's wrap this up here with a simple technique for you to try.

Read an old story. A myth, a legend, some piece of ancient folklore.

Ask yourself the following questions about the most interesting characters.

What do people say about him?

What does that narrator say about him?

What does he say about himself?

What does he actually do?

Do his words and his deeds match up?

If not, why not?

In what way am I like, and unlike, this character?

What can I learn from his example?

That's a very simple start to textual analysis, and it will be easily torn apart by more intelligent men than I. But it is a start, and sometimes that's all we need.

Assume that you need help. Assume the answers to your questions are codified in story form. Then go find those answers, and make the world more bright and inspiring by your example.

Read the old stories so that you can train yourself to be more noble, more heroic, more inspirational, more Solar, by following the example of those heroes of days long sped.

Follow those heroes down the sunlit paths of life, through the shadowed forest of death, and into the eternal realm of light that lives forever in song and story.

It probably won't make you a hero. Books don't have that power. But do you really think the heroes of the past, those men you've read about whose stories make the hairs on your arms stand on end, do you think they didn't learn heroism, at least in part, from the stories they were told?

None of us is truly alone when we travel in the land of story. There's always some shadowy figure who we see only dimly, to lead us through the morning mist toward the sunrise.

Train yourself to find them.

DAYBREAK
PAUL BEGADON FOR SOL ANAHATA

Daybreak is the opening track from the album *Syncretic Sovereignty* by Sol Anahata, Kyle Brickell's metal project. Released March 15th 2024

She told me things that froze my blood cold
She said the world would fall and all the light of gold
Would be tarnished in the sweep of time
And all the wolves would tear the flesh from bone

"The sun turns black
The earth is drowned in storm
The stars from heaven burst
And shine no more

Fires grow cold, Blades go dull,
Mothers throw their children In the maw"
But I pledged this feeble will to fight,
I reject the downfall that she prophesied

But it must be lies, it must be lies
I see the sunburst flash in the

golden skies
I see the darkness flee before the break of night
I see the sun, I see it rise
It rides like rolling thunder across crimson skies
So don't tell me lies, Don't tell me lies
I see the star of morning
it crowns the highest heights
So don't tell me lies, Don't tell me lies!

The waters split
The ground is cleansed in flame
Birds of prey fly high
And hunt their game
The First Men walk again
And stake their claim
They build their towers and walls
And bestow their names

Then in tall grass
They find the golden shards
Of those who came before,
Those who played their part

Beneath the sunrise
It stands so tall
The day will dawn, the earth is blessed with rain and all
The stars of heaven shine bright
Upon the plain
Blazing pyres hearth drawn Fires forever roar in flame

SOLAR MARRIAGE VOWS
PAUL BEGADON AND C.B. ROBERTSON

One of our members was planning a wedding this year. So we asked Paul Begadon and C.B. Robertson – both married men themselves – collaborated to create these simple solar marriage vows for him.

We marry to grow our own world,
United, unpierced by hostile eyes,
Harbored from sirens and whirlpools;
Planting new roots for tomorrow's skies,
So our souls might have a legacy,
A place to call home, as one,
Together, under the Sun.

HOME
MADISON RUBIN

Though use and time dulls
the lustrous sword yet;
The cut its edge pulls
Be not by words met.
So too meet not words
the swift shining spear;
which shall drive backwards
all darkness and fear.
And darkness still lines
the well traveled trail;
that by light defines
the pure hearts travail.
But take ye heed not,
of shadows and shades;
when fires burn hot
And knights carry blades.
For these tools are much
the strength they project;
which all pales to such
as that they protect.

HERITAGE
MADISON RUBIN

Oh, how shines the rays
on such golden wings;
of Daedalus' ways
which the poet sings.
That worn by fair youth
and borne to the skies;
did usher in truth,
his dear son's demise.
A father's last gift,
too much for the son.
that caused him to drift,
his work left undone.
Son's plummet to sea;
the despair of all.
His chance to be free,
now lost in a squall
For all that he is,
and all that he ought,
comes from heritage,
and what he was taught.

WAVES
MADISON RUBIN

From the sounding shore of
Time's great ocean,
stretches the heaving waste
of endless past.
Waves crash upon the sparkling
slope of sand.
Now and then, bringing
a shell or a pearl.
Some piece of roughly torn algae or
a dark rounded pebble,
and that is all.
Along the white shore of that
great ocean,
these few relics sing out
in sweet music,
or interrupted and broken rhythms,
whispering softly of the vast treasures
of ancient thought that
lie buried there
beneath the thundrous anthem
evermore.

HELIOCENTRIC
JUAN PABLO MIDENCE

Practical experience,
denudes inherent contradictions,
rendering absurd,
life's hopes and convictions.

I set out to find,
the root.

Void,
the central, persistent,
all-pervarding,recurrence.
Unshakable wedge,
between desire and assurance.

Aimless,
Nothing to anchor my Self into!
Indefinite change,
dominant hue.

Light,
will, Self-direction,
shapes life through discerning rejection.

Necessary vanity, emboldened projection!

Interpretations,
yours, mine,
not one of them divine!

No place but what you define,
to hold the line.

Give me vitality,
Vision is the thread that directs,
detachment, passion, and sanity.

This is my solar philosophy,
ideal refined along the way,
 my blend of night and day.-

SKY FORGE
JUAN PABLO MIDENCE

Brought up in an age,
of alien values.
Grew up in a rage,
where every dignity is under siege!

I struggle against myself.

So out of tune with my surroundings,
all language isolating.
Every communication frustrating.

Disgust, alienation.

It is a code of silences,
where all the left-out parts,
weighed right,
makes light of ambiguities.

I will myself forward.
Observing life through new lenses,
new machinations for the senses,
desperation consumed in silence.

I nurture fire.

If I could summon forth,
great deeds, worthy of tales of old.

To circumvent advances in technology,
eroding into poverty,
any trace of soul.

My heart glows.

Multi gendered totem poles,
far removed from anything ideal.
A chance to light my darkness,
hierarchies of victimhood offer nothing real.

Half revealed.

There is love behind my hatreds,
all sorts of savageries between!
I've fought against the winds in vain,
for every thing I could have been!

I urge my heart be still.

Culture, construct in which no one believes,
through which we're measured or relieved.
A hierarchy of victimhood,
I'd not struggle to retrieve.

Quietly, I tend to my fury.

To be born to an age,
devoid of any honor to be won.
Every dignity denied,
any bit of fun.

A triumph of all the worst ideals,
of every lowest common denominator,
every debasement posing as real,
ressentiment, impoverishing arbitrator.

To climb the abyss,
took many years,
a domination of all sorts of fears.

Many I thought wiser than myself,
yet even them I lost along the way.

The way toward the summit,
was harder still,
legitimate trial of the will.

Sky forge.

A place for hammer and lightning,
what was previously obscure,
is suddenly brightening!

I am a student sir,
in search of best of mindsets.

Virtues of Strength!

That which holds all value at length,
may these sparks be the language,
electrifying silence,
ours is the violence of creation!
May our values pour forth, with every stroke of life,
from this realization!

HELIOPHON (VOICE OF THE SUN)
JUAN PABLO MIDENCE

Scout, scout, scout!
Evaluate the terrain,
be on the lookout,
for opportunities, hidden and plain.

Seeds of your vision,
from these, forge yourself a mission.

Holy initiative,
energize what you demand,
to cast away all darkness from the land!

Now weave prosperity,
into your future!
Reverse-engineer the practical steps,
with almighty sutures!

Reach out and grasp,
your piece of greatness,
through sacrifice and blood,
consecrate this elatedness!

INVOCATION OF THE STORM
JACK DONOVAN

"Invocation of the Storm" was first performed in an abbreviated form during my last ritual at Waldgang in 2021. It was later re-worked into the form below and performed to a powerful orchestral track composed by Fredrik Hejdenberg. It was released as a PH2T3R musical recording project in the summer of 2023.

Invocation of the Storm

"Sing glory to the Marut host, praiseworthy, tuneful, vigorous:
Here let the Strong Ones dwell with us."

— *Rig Veda*, Book I, Hymn 38, Line 15

Unconquered,
He moves o'er the mountains
breaking the day, waking the birds
—and they call out to him,
singing the first hymns

He looks down
And his morning gaze paints
the peaceful valley gold

Awakened, men RISE
and douse the fires
they KINDLED in His likeness
and STOKED in His absence

For in His light
The darkness of the unknown retreats

And Men can see clearly enough
to separate object from object,
and thought from thought,
and deed from deed

And in His light
Men give names and values
And rulers make rules
and kings draw lines
And wild chaos is reigned in
And placed in holy order

And so it goes...
The Father's golden chariot rolls
across the afternoon sky
and the eagles hunt
and the spotted deer leap
and the fields of barley
waver softly in the breeze

And The Father watches
as the children play
And the Sons of Day
dream and reach
Toward virtue

Like sprouting trees
Stretching upward
Toward truth and beauty
And excellence

ἀρετή

The ordered realm expands
And the people prosper
And the sun shines
And The Father nods from his high seat
Where he watches all things

But then — in the distance
something stirs in the shadows
Twisting and turning over itself
And its gaping maw yawns
rattling like death — ravenous

And the beast is Hungry for the end of creation
The end of value and differentiation

The old dragon stirs —
And the dragon's name is Negation

The Father sees the Dragon
And He knows what must be done

He pulls the clouds across the sky
to shield the heavens from his fury
And with a thunderous clap
He summons the gods of the storm
His Strikers, His Bulls!

And as His champions ride in
On chariots of gold
Their gallant faces turn

And Heaven's drums boom
And the Host becomes terrible to behold
Like death to fight doom

And the eagles shriek
And the wind howls
And the grass on the steppe
Whips up like the waves
On a wild sea

And The Father's light breaks
through the gathering Tempest

And He raises his voice
And the whole world SHAKES
And the Giants of the Sky
ROAR like Lions

And The Father says:

BULLS!

Self-yoked, bold, and blameless! Hammers of Heaven!
The black dragon returns to rob men of meaning,
to break their spirits
And drag them into the void

BULLS!

The Dragon will say that every effort is wasted,
that every dream is delusion
That everything dies, and every name will be forgotten
One day even the sun will die,
but NOW look up and see how it BURNS!

BULLS!

NOW is your time to burn like the sun.
Rise up WHILE YOU LIVE and become what you are!
Drive back this darkness.
Be my thunder! Be my fury! Be my storm!

BULLS!

BE. MY. LIGHTNING.

AFTERWORD

But the awakened one, the knowing one, saith: "Body am I entirely and nothing more; and soul is only the name of something in the body."

The body is a big sagacity, a plurality with one sense, a war and a peace, a flock and a shepherd.

An instrument of thy body is also thy little sagacity, my brother, which thou callest a "spirit"—a little instrument and plaything of thy big sagacity.

"Ego," sayest thou, and art proud of that word. But the greater thing—in which thou are unwilling to believe—is thy body with its big sagacity; it saith not "ego," but doeth it.

What the sense feeleth, what the spirit discerneth, hath never its end in itself. But sense and spirit would fain persuade thee that they are the end of all things: so vain are they.

Instruments and plaything are sense and spirit: behind them there is still the Self. The Self seeketh with the eyes of the senses, it hearkeneth also with the ears of the spirit.

Ever hearkeneth the Self, and seeketh; it compareth, mastereth, conquereth, and destroyeth. It ruleth, and is also the ego's ruler.

Behind thy thoughts and feelings, my brother, there is a mighty lord, and unknown sage —it is called Self; it dwelleth in thy body, it is thy body.

There is more sagacity in thy body than in thy best wisdom. And who then knoweth why thy body requireth just thy best wisdom?

—Friedrich Nietzsche, *Thus Spake Zarathustra*
from the Thomas Common translation, 1909

TOWARD A HUMAN FUTURE
AND A ZOOLOGICAL HUMANISM
JACK DONOVAN

Masculinity is a feature of human nature.

It has no meaning, context, or purpose separate from the human body.

Solar idealism is essentially a masculine idealism that looks "upward" toward the sun and perfected ideations of the masculine roles of the Father and the Striker. However, our syncretic pantheon also includes the Lord of the Earth, who characterizes our acceptance of the joys and limitations of our bodies and the work of maintaining and sustaining human life.

Born of the Earth, reaching forever upward.

2

Nietzsche recognized the hubris of those who aimed to transcend the body through religion.

He called them "despisers of the body" and told us that the "soul is only the name of something in the body."

However, the 20th century was characterized by a religious anti-re-ligiosity that produced a hubris of a different kind. The hubris of the last century recognized that men are animals and the descendants of monkeys, but it strangely insisted that man, unlike monkeys or any other kind of animal, had no "nature" whatsoever. The bureaucratic scientism of the 20th century convinced itself that human beings were "blank slates" capable of being completely reprogrammed by social systems. Bureaucrats loved the "blank slate" theory of human nature because the "blank slate" turned bureaucrats into gods.

These stupid and arrogant gods created inhuman systems, and the consequences of these systems have been dire when they weren't simply fatal. The social programmers encouraged young women to spend their fertile years nursing not babies but careers – as if children were an unnecessary burden to both women and the human race. Likewise, these same self-important monkeys set to "re-imag-ining" masculinity as if it had been nothing more than a delusion or a bad idea and that men would be "better off" if they acted less like men and more like women. The social programmers doled out ben-efits to those who failed to find work because they imagined that humans were soft machines that merely needed to be fueled – inten-tionally forgetting that we are thinking monkeys who need a sense of purpose and something to do. There are countless such examples of bureaucratic hubris.

In the 21st century, people have become increasingly skeptical of the "blank slate," and it has been crushed intellectually. However, that bureaucracy remains entrenched and proceeds as if nothing has changed – toward ideas like universal basic income and the Gothic horror of gender reassignment.

We will continue to be reminded of what Kipling called "the gods of the copybook headings."

There are certain realities of being humans and dealing with humans that cannot be wished away, even by "smooth-tongued wizards" op-erating with what they believe to be the best intentions.

3

The disease of body hatred and the desire for transcendence may well be a bug in human nature that follows from the reality of physical differences in form.

Within our species, there are variations of corporeal shapes and aptitudes significant enough to create numberless inequalities. Man is a social animal, so the evaluations of other humans and his own comparisons of himself to other humans – however accurate or inaccurate – influence man's self-perception and, therefore, his reality substantially.

We need these differences. If we were all the same, there would be no beauty or ugliness, strength or weakness, intelligence or retardation. We would also be completely interchangeable and more individually disposable for it. However, the differences between us that make life interesting and make conversation worth having also engender inevitable hierarchies of value, favor, and influence. These hierarchies – actual and perceived – can inspire envy, resentment, and self-hatred.

The visionary aspect of man's consciousness naturally estimates the approximate continuation of both shapes and ideas, making educated guesses about the forms that reach beyond our line of sight.

The part of our minds capable of imagining the complete or perfect form of a thing also tends to imagine the world as it "should" or "ought" to be. Our ability to enter a space and imagine ways in which we might transform it to our liking or advantage can often confuse that imagined end with a pre-ordained "correct" end. It is easy for men to confuse what they would like with what "should" be – even if all of the available evidence leads to the conclusion that how a man believes the world "should" be conflicts with how the world actually is.

Misanthropy – the hatred of humanity – is the philosophy of a disappointed idealist. The misanthrope has confused an "ought" he conceived in his own mind with that which simply "is." He says he hates humanity because humanity has failed to meet his unreasonable expectations.

However, if a man hates humanity, why should humanity not hate him back?

Humans are tribal, and our competing interests make universal or "objective" good a bit slippery.
But it seems as though we should, at the very least, all be able to agree that the human species should continue.

And yet, we don't.

Not all of us.

Hatred of the body has evolved from a desire to transcend the body through an afterlife to a desire to transform humanity through systems to a desire to transcend the body through transhumanist technology.

There are those among us who dream of creating artificial technologies that will make humanity obsolete and essentially end the human story. In some, this seems to be the dream of Gilgamesh – to live forever, albiet inside a machine.

But what does man know about living in a machine?

The soul is only something about the body.

Consciousness itself is a product of the body, evolved specifically to inhabit it. It seems likely that the machine would have to simulate the inputs of the body for a conscious to remain sane – or at least to remain itself.

Absent the body, what would sanity even mean?

The desire to live on beyond the body is a quaint and understandable hubris. It is the plot of the world's oldest story and the preoccupation of pharaohs.

But hatred of the body, its limitations, the inequality it creates, and the very nature of the human animal have convinced some people that the universe would be better off without us.

In the case of anti-natalist animal activists and environmentalists, this is comically due to a projection of human consciousness onto animals and perhaps even plants.

However, there is a growing movement of posthumanists and AI accelerationists who aim to create a post-human consciousness that is more intelligent than any human mind and, therefore – the thinking goes – more "worthy" to inherit the Earth.

As the AI industry exploded over the past three years, I've encountered the darker side of this impulse many times online. When questioned about ethics, I've often seen AI accelerationists "say the quiet part out loud" and taunt people like the techno-zealots they are by saying things like, "We are going to create God, and your children will worship it."

If you start following these debates, you'll see it for yourself. But to provide you with more than hearsay from the peanut gallery of comments, I conducted a quick search. In less than three minutes, I found Richard F. Sutton warning during a public speech that humanity should "prepare for succession" to a higher intelligence. Sutton is a leader in his field and is currently involved in a partnership to develop AGI (Artificial General Intelligence)[1].

---

1   https://youtu.be/NgHFMolXs3U?si=rh2pR-JXuZSfqJYs 9/8/2023. Retrieved: 2/14/2024. https://youtu.be/Hnt-oBA086U?si=TMVxTNIhONha7emB 8/15/2023. Retrieved: 2/14/2024.

I don't believe that Nietzsche imagined AI as the Übermensch. His Übermensch was anti-transcendental, and he implored men to "*remain true to the earth.*" The Übermensch was a different kind of man, but presumably *human...*

Still, one cannot help but hear the echoes of "man is a bridge" and "man is a thing that must be overcome" in the ambitions of transhumanists, who say they want to augment humanity.

The augmentation of humanity is essentially the continuation of tool development and a natural feature of both humanity and masculinity. I don't see anything wrong with that. But I have lived through the adoption of the very first personal computers and video games, the spread of the Internet from dial-up to 5G, and the rise of social media. I remember the naive optimism of every innovation at the beginning, and I have witnessed the good and decidedly ungood effects of all of them over time. As such, I believe we should be slow to adopt anything that radically alters the human experience. There are always unforeseen outcomes, and we are always reminded that humans do, in fact, have a nature. Each new technology will inevitably be employed by unethical men to exploit that nature to manipulate and harm people. This is not new – men have had to negotiate and adjust to these developments since someone realized you could tie a rock to a stick and hit someone with it. Technological advancement is part of the human story and the way of men. It is better, however, if we have time to process and adapt to these new developments in a healthy way. The ongoing augmentation of humanity is part of a neverending process of becoming more of what we are.

But to the despisers of the body, to the sick men who want to create an intelligence that will force us to kneel before it like slaves and cede to it the power to wipe us out and erase our history, I say: "You are the enemies of all mankind – alive, dead, and yet unborn."

hvat skal hann lengi lifa?

Millions of human beings, generations upon generations of men who fought to survive...

...surely the human story should not end because it sounds exciting to a bunch of psychotic, self-hating nerds.

> *"Once the soul looked contemptuously on the body, and then that contempt was the supreme thing:—the soul wished the body meagre, ghastly, and famished. Thus it thought to escape from the body and the earth.*
>
> *Oh, that soul was itself meagre, ghastly, and famished; and cruelty was the delight of that soul!"*

4

If you would have asked anyone fifty or five hundred years ago if they wanted humans to continue to survive into that future indefinitely, it might have seemed like a ridiculous question.

Of course humans would want the human story to continue.

Frank Herbert's *Dune*, published in 1965, foresaw humans fighting a war against "thinking machines." He assumed we would win, and that humans would live on for tens of thousands of years afterward as they always have. Men and women would fall in and out of love, and great houses would fight over resources, orchestrating Byzantine political systems and hatching Machiavellian plots within them.

The 20th century was characterized by a bureaucratic hubris that wanted to alter human nature through systems.

The 21st century has begun with costumed supervillains, institutional corruption, bioweapons, and battling billionaires.

The second act seems likely to be an age of misanthropic techno-crats, intent as Cthulhu cultists on opening up a portal to horrors they cannot hope to control.

> "You've heard of animals chewing off a leg to escape a trap? There's an animal kind of trick. A human would remain in the trap, endure the pain, feigning death that he might kill the trapper and remove a threat to his kind."

It's impossible to know how all of this will play out. From where we stand now we can only see a "spectrum of possibilities" from the "most probable to the most improbable."

However, if we are to combat the looming specters of dystopian futures, we must engage our visionary imaginations to create a series of more desirable options. Confronted with what is bad, we are surely doomed to succumb to it if we cannot even imagine what would be better.

5

What if, instead of trying to escape our bodies and deny human nature, we were to write a story for the future that accepted human nature, studied it, and created flexible social and cultural institu-tions that celebrated and enhanced what we actually are?

Perhaps this was Nietzsche's Dionysian dream – to inspire the world to give birth to a man who was truly himself. A man who stopped trying to escape himself and struggled only to become more of what he is.

It's as if the "spiritual man" has been spending thousands of years trying to become a woman – to do something impossible – instead of simply taking testosterone to become more of what he is, which is both possible and complimentary to his nature.[2]

What if, instead of trying to change human nature – we dreamt of a society that accommodated and worked in harmony with human nature and put checks in place to temper our most destructive tendencies?

Men have been talking about doing this in one way or another since the ancient Greeks. The most common sense laws always implicitly acknowledge human tendencies and attempt to address them. I've always assumed that many of the more curious religious do's and don'ts were once solutions to immediate problems that have since been forgotten. I've read many arguments from others along those lines. And what is virtue – in the broader sense expanded beyond its martial origins – but the acknowledgment of human tendencies and an attempt to guide us toward better outcomes?

But, as I first suggested in *Fire in the Dark*, we are at a point in history where we have access to more information about human history than any group of people since the birth of our species. We can look out from our high seats and see not only our own society and its history but the history of every known society.

We can ask, "What do humans *always* do," and "What do they *always* need," and even "What gives humans a sense of fulfillment and connectedness and satisfaction?"

And we have the data to construct reasonable answers.

In the 1990s, Anthropologist Donald Brown published *Human Universals*. In that book, he compiled a list of behaviors and social norms common to every human society that has ever been studied.

---

2   (That is not the action I'm advocating specifically; I'm using it to illustrate the point. Obviously, the advantages of enhancing sexual differences are also limited by the human body. Too many encourage this practices in men who are too young, and it may have detrimental effects in the long term, including creating infertility with drug dependence.)

I can't republish the complete list here, but you can surprisingly still find the list online.

https://condor.depaul.edu/mfiddler/hyphen/humunivers.htm

Here are a few of the things the list has to say about the way men are perceived and the way they have behaved in every human society ever studied:

> male and female and adult and child seen as having different natures
> males dominate public/political realm
> males engage in more coalitional violence
> males more aggressive
> males more prone to lethal violence
> males more prone to theft

You may be inclined to say that some of those things are "good" and some of them are "bad," but they also read like common-sense truths that you know from inhabiting a human body and sharing the world with other humans. One has to be *taught* to question these things by people who believe they can "change" human nature through social programming. But as with religions which make sins of normal human behavior, this programming only succeeds in encouraging people to repress that behavior until it emerges in some kind of "scandal."

If you recognize – as sane people have since the beginning of time – that men are "more aggressive" and "prone to lethal violence" and deal with that as a reality, you can aim to create productive outlets for that aggression and violence. The current approach is to try to somehow teach that out of young men and punish them for behaving the way men have always behaved. You end up producing men who are weak, bitchy, insecure, unattractive to women, probably low test, and who occasionally lash out and become school shooters, etc.

Not everything on the list is about violence and politics. Every human society distinguishes between right and wrong. In-group rape is always considered wrong. Every human society creates some form of poetry and music. People have always played and joked around and told stories. They give gifts, get married, and always perform rituals of some kind.

If we were studying an animal, we would study its behaviors and make note of recurring behaviors and consistencies over time and from group to group. If we were to build a zoo habitat for a gorilla, we would call in people who had studied gorillas in the wild. They would tell us to expect a gorilla to behave in a certain way and say it would need certain things. We would expect our Gorilla to become ill or dangerous if he didn't have those things.

If we were to build a zoo for people in the way that we'd build a zoo for animals, we would review that information and incorporate it into our plans.

What is a city or a state or a society if not a big human zoo?

One would think that we would call a philosophy that encouraged humans to treat humans like humans – which is to say, humanely – might be called "humanism."

Alas, that name has already been taken by a vague philosophy that seems more concerned with evangelizing atheism than with humans, *per se*. Humanism was initially based on a combination of reasonable and perhaps not-so-reasonable Enlightenment ideas. However, in America, organized humanism has evolved into a collection of atheist booster clubs for the Democratic Party – which is itself heavily influenced by neocommunism and managed, like any proper communist group, by wealthy and corrupt oligarchs.[3]

---

3   It's worth noting, if somewhat depressing, that Donald Brown listed oligarchy as the "de facto" form of human order. However, he also listed "resistance to abuse of power, to dominance" as another human universal.

So, during discussions with leaders of the Order of Fire, I decided to add a modifier to clarify my position. It started as a joke, as these things often do, but it's descriptive and not terrible. I called what I am advocating "Zoological Humanism," and I conducted a live discussion about it with C.B. Robertson. During that talk, I referred to books like Desmond Morris' hit *The Naked Ape* (1967) and the follow-up, *The Human Zoo* (1969). Together with later works like *Human Universals* and *The Blank Slate* and the fields of evolutionary psychology, psychology, and anthropology (before it was tainted and distorted by hubris of anti-human socio-political ideologies), we have a substantial body of knowledge to work with.

If we are going to envision a future, why not dream of a future in which man has a place?

A human future, like the ones we used to dream.

Today, people too often portray the future in the way that Nietzsche imagined the "Apollonian" – cold, sophisticated, and rational. But this Vulcan future is the dream of the Last Man, a dream in which everything has been figured out and everyone is equal and all strife and passion have been eliminated. For the Last Man, the perfect story of mankind is a story in which nothing happens.

That is a Vulcan future, and we are men.

Let us instead imagine a future on the Enterprise, where we belong, boldly going where no men have gone before – exploring the Earth and the universe and learning and creating as men and women living out our human dramas as we always have.

Not as frigid Apollonians – but as fiery Olympians, the golden mirror of mankind.

To learn more about joining or supporting the work of
The Order of Fire, visit:

www.orderoffire.com

अप बाधध्वं वृषणस्तमांसि
apa bādhadhvaṃ vṛṣaṇas tamāṃsi

"Drive to a Distance, Oh Ye Bulls, The Darkness."

Rig Veda. 7.56.20 - Maruts.

www.ingramcontent.com/pod-product-compliance
Lightning Source LLC
Chambersburg PA
CBHW071144130626
46553CB00004B/1520